WATERFRONT PORCH

WATERFRONT

PORCH

RECLAIMING DETROIT'S
INDUSTRIAL WATERFRONT AS
A GATHERING PLACE FOR ALL

John H. Hartig

Greenstone Books | *East Lansing*

∞ The paper used in this publication meets the minimum requirements
of ANSI/NISO Z39.48-1992 (R 1997) (Permanence of Paper).

Greenstone Books
East Lansing, Michigan 48823-5245

Michigan State University Press
East Lansing, Michigan 48823-5245

The mission of Greenstone Books—a name chosen to evoke
the state gem of Michigan—is to publish works in history and
environmental studies accessible to a general readership.

Printed and bound in the United States of America.

28 27 26 25 24 23 22 21 20 19   1 2 3 4 5 6 7 8 9 10

Library of Congress Control Number: 2018939762
ISBN: 978-1-948314-02-2 (pbk.)
ISBN: 978-1-948314-03-9 (ebook: PDF)

Book design by Charlie Sharp, Sharp Des!gns, East Lansing, Michigan
Cover design by Erin Kirk New
Cover photo of the Detroit RiverWalk by Ken Cobb.

Michigan State University Press is a member of the Green Press Initiative and is
committed to developing and encouraging ecologically responsible publishing
practices. For more information about the Green Press Initiative and the use of
recycled paper in book publishing, please visit *www.greenpressinitiative.org*.

Visit Michigan State University Press at *www.msupress.org*

Contents

vii   FOREWORD

xi   ACKNOWLEDGMENTS

1   PROLOGUE

9   CHAPTER 1. Detroit's History in Addressing Paradigm Shifts

33   CHAPTER 2. Historical Changes in the Riverfront

55   CHAPTER 3. Detroit River Revival

77   CHAPTER 4. Forging the Detroit RiverWalk

119   CHAPTER 5. Place-Making in the D

141   CHAPTER 6. Greenways, Blueways, and Flyways

159   CHAPTER 7. Economic Benefits

175   CHAPTER 8. Why Care about the Revitalization of Detroit?

195   CHAPTER 9. Lessons Learned and the Future

213   EPILOGUE

219   REFERENCES

231   INDEX

Foreword

Mark C. Wallace

n 2003, a visionary group of leaders came together to transform Detroit's blighted industrial waterfront into the Detroit RiverWalk. The nonprofit Detroit RiverFront Conservancy was started with three simple promises: we promised the community that we would be a good steward of the riverfront, that the RiverWalk would be world-class, and that the riverfront would always be a place where everyone is welcome and everyone would be respected. Today, the Detroit RiverWalk is the most diverse gathering space in the state of Michigan. People come to the riverfront for recreation. People come to the riverfront to interact with nature. People come to the riverfront to escape the stress of the city. And people come to the riverfront because they know it's a place where they will be respected. More than three million people per year come to the Detroit RiverWalk, and they come from all walks of life. The Detroit RiverWalk has taught our community how to come together. This gives me great hope for our future.

Since joining the Detroit RiverFront Conservancy as president and chief executive officer in 2014, I have had the opportunity to work with some amazing leaders. In this role, I am keenly aware that the success of the Detroit RiverWalk stands on the shoulders of many people. Before the Conservancy started building the RiverWalk, a small group of dedicated people began working to improve the quality of the Detroit River. Without this early focus on water quality, the transformation of the river's edge would not have been possible. This group of advocates were dedicated experts who showed tremendous collaboration in attacking a complex problem to restore water quality.

At every step of the way, Dr. John Hartig has provided outstanding leadership. He is the singular individual who stewarded both the restoration of the waterway and the transformation of the river's edge. Dr. Hartig is beloved, and every time you mention his name in the world of ecology or environmental science, people start to smile and say something along the lines of "John Hartig is the best guy in the world." His success with this work demonstrates his tenacity, his expertise, and his charisma as a leader.

When I took the position as president and chief executive officer of the Detroit RiverFront Conservancy, I quickly clicked with John Hartig, professionally and personally. We have worked closely together ever since. John is easy to admire, and he is an amazing colleague.

John was raised in metropolitan Detroit and acquired a love for the outdoors while canoeing on Belle Isle, fishing in the Detroit River, and vacationing in northern Michigan each summer. That passion for the outdoors and an interest in the cleanup of the Detroit River and Great Lakes led him to a thirty-year career as an award-winning Great Lakes scientist and conservationist.

During the late 1970s and early 1980s, John was involved in water quality monitoring of the Detroit River in support of pollution control efforts. Starting in the mid-1980s and through the late 1990s, he worked for the International Joint Commission where he was instrumental in establishing the remedial action plan program for cleaning up polluted areas of the Great Lakes, called Areas of Concern, including the Detroit River. He then was selected in 1999 to become river navigator for the Greater Detroit American Heritage River Initiative, established by presidential executive order, where he championed environmental stewardship, environmentally sustainable economic development, and historical and cultural preservation. One of the top priorities of this initiative was linked greenways. While river navigator, he was appointed in 2002 to the city of Detroit's "Blue Ribbon Committee" that called for the creation of the Detroit RiverWalk and establishment of the Detroit RiverFront Conservancy. In 2003, he was appointed as a founding member of the Detroit RiverFront Conservancy and continues to serve in that capacity today. Then in 2004, he was appointed as the first refuge manager of the Detroit River International Wildlife Refuge that has championed regional and international connections and reconnecting people with nature to inspire the next generation of conservationists and sustainability entrepreneurs. As you can see, John Hartig and the Detroit River go hand in hand.

John is also a prolific writer who has authored or coauthored more than one hundred scientific publications and four books: *Bringing Conservation to Cities*; *Burning Rivers*; *Honoring Our Detroit River: Caring for Our Home*; and *Under RAPs: Toward Grassroots Ecological Democracy in the Great Lakes Basin*. John's most recent book, *Bringing Conservation to Cities*, won a gold medal from the Nonfiction Authors Association in the "Sustainable Living" category and a bronze medal from the Living Now Book Awards in the "Green Living" category. John has also received numerous awards for his work, including the 2017 Community Peacemaker Award from Wayne State University's Center for Peace and Conflict Studies, the 2016 Edward G. Voss Conservation Science Award from the Michigan Nature Association, the 2015 Conservationist of the Year Award from the John Muir Association, the 2013 Conservation Advocate of the Year Award from the Michigan League of Conservation Voters, and a 2010 Green Leaders' Award from the *Detroit Free Press*.

In many respects, John's career has evolved from scientist through science translator to award-winning, creative, nonfiction writer focused on inspiring the next generation of conservationists and sustainability entrepreneurs in urban areas because that is now where most people live. But it is his extensive knowledge, long-term involvement, and effective communication skills that make him uniquely qualified to tell this *Waterfront Porch* story that will inspire others to get involved and will give hope throughout the world. As you can see, there is no better person to tell this story of reclaiming Detroit's industrial waterfront as a gathering place for all.

If you love Detroit and care about its future, you must read *Waterfront Porch*. If you are interested in sustainable redevelopment, urban waterfront revitalization, reconnecting people with nature, successful public–private partnerships, or place-making for all, then this book is a must read.

Waterfront Porch is a timely narrative of the origins and efforts to build the Detroit RiverWalk, complete with lessons learned. I highly recommend *Waterfront Porch* to you because it shows how we can successfully undertake waterfront place-making for people and wildlife, and that we can do it in a fashion that brings out the best in all of us.

Acknowledgments

Waterfront Porch is the story of thousands of people, organizations, and businesses coming together to vision, plan, fund, program, and steward the Detroit RiverWalk. I personally have been so inspired by these people, organizations, and businesses who have come together to create a waterfront gathering place for all that contributes to the revitalization of Detroit, changes the perception of the place we all call home, and is a gift to future generations. Clearly, this book would not have been possible without their significant contributions. I would like to specifically acknowledge:

- the Blue Ribbon Committee established in 2002 to transform the Detroit riverfront;
- all the members, past and present, of the Board of Directors of the Detroit RiverFront Conservancy;
- the staff, past and present, of the Detroit RiverFront Conservancy who have facilitated and guided the process, made sure that all

stakeholders feel appreciated, and consistently delivered on-time, within budget, and with quality;

- the foundations, businesses, firms, agencies, and individuals who have made the Detroit RiverWalk possible with generous gifts and grants; and

- the numerous individuals, too many to count, who have dared to believe that their efforts could make a difference and help create a waterfront destination of choice for all.

This book was written, in part, during a writing residency at Write On, Door County in Fish Creek, Wisconsin. I gratefully acknowledge that unique opportunity to write without interruption in such an inspirational location. I also would like to thank the Detroit RiverFront Conservancy for the honor of serving on its Board of Directors from its inception and to thank the Community Foundation for Southeast Michigan for underwriting this book to make it affordable.

I would also like to thank Julie Loehr, Editor of Michigan State University Press, and all her staff for their encouragement and help, and their unique contributions to the production and marketing process. Finally, I would like to especially thank my family for their continued support of my work and for their understanding of my passion for environmental writing that accelerates the sustainability transition.

Prologue

When most people think of Detroit they think about automobiles, Motown, or professional sports. However, Detroit has an incredibly rich history, starting with Native Americans who lived along the Detroit River and in its watershed for thousands of years. Along the Detroit River, the Algonquins were early inhabitants (Cornell 2003). They located along the Detroit River because of the incredible natural resource base and because the river served as an efficient transportation route. These Algonquins hunted along its shore and in its marshes, fished it, transported people and food on it, buried their ancestors next to it, and gathered on the water's edge for celebrations and ceremonies. They used the word *Wawiiatanong* to refer to the place along the river where they had their earliest historical village (Cornell 2003). *Wawiiatanong* literally means "the place on the curve or bend."

In the 1600s, French explorers came to the Great Lakes Basin ecosystem looking to expand their empire. They first came looking for a natural waterway up the St. Lawrence River, through the Great Lakes, and down the Mississippi River to New Orleans, and hoped that this crescent-shaped transportation route would become the central avenue of communication for a new France (Hatcher 1945). The first sail of a European across Lake Erie and up the Detroit River was by a thirty-five-year old French explorer named Robert de La Salle in 1679. As was customary during that time, a priest was onboard to minister to the captain and crew. The priest was named Father Louis Hennepin who recorded his observations and sentiments at that time:

> The straight is finer than that of Niagara, being thirty leagues long, and everywhere one league broad, except in the middle which is wider, forming the Lake we have named St. Clair. The navigation is easy on both sides, the coast being low and even. It runs directly north to south. The country between these two lakes is very well situated and the soil very fertile. The banks of the straight are vast meadows, and the prospect is terminated with some hills covered with vineyards, trees bearing good fruit, groves and forests so well disposed that one would think nature alone could not have made, without the help of art so charming a prospect. The country is stocked with stags, wild goats, and bears which are good for food, and not fierce as in other countries. (Hatcher 1945, 33-34)

The first French settlement in Detroit was established by a French officer named Antoine de la Mothe Cadillac in 1701, seventy-five years before the founding of the United States (figure 1). Cadillac's vision was to establish a strong French post at a strategic location in the narrows of the Detroit River that would be a bulwark against the British traders, a center of influence among the Native Americans, and a key bastion in

FIGURE 1. (opposite) Early French depiction of the Detroit River and the plan for Fort Detroit.

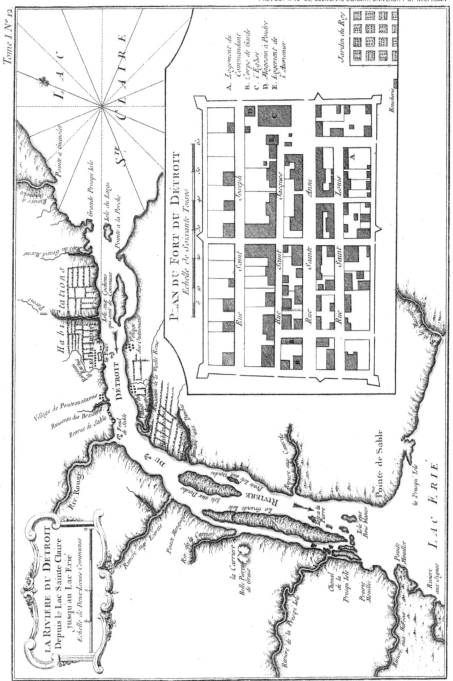

Tome I Nº 12

LAC STE CLAIRE

A. Logement du Commandant
B. Corps de Garde
C. l'Eglise
D. Magasin à Poudre
E. Logement de l'Aumonier

Jardin du Rey

PLAN DU FORT DU DÉTROIT
Echelle de Soixante Toises

Rue Sainct Joseph

Rue Sainct Jacques

Rue Sainte Anne

Rue Saint Louis

Boucherie

LA RIVIERE DU DÉTROIT
Depuis le Lac Sainte Claire
Jusqu'au Lac Erie
Echelle de Deux Lieües Communes

LAC ERIE

the chain of forts from Quebec to the lower Mississippi (Hatcher 1945). In French, the word *detroit* means "narrows" or "straight."

Through early exploration, the French discovered that the Great Lakes and the Detroit River watershed had plenty of beaver. Soon French-Canadian *voyageurs* in birchbark canoes, trappers, and traders came in search of fur trading opportunities. Today, it is widely recognized that the outpost at Detroit became a strategic move in protecting French trapping interests. Clearly, Detroit was founded in response to the fur trade and went on to become a major processer and exporter of furs during the fur trade era.

In the years following European settlement, there was a necessary shift in societal focus from one dominated by hunting and gathering to one practicing farming, lumbering, and more trading. Detroit's commerce and industry then took a great leap forward with the completion of the Erie Canal in 1825. For example, the cost of transporting a barrel of goods from Detroit to Buffalo, New York, decreased from five dollars in 1815 to fifty cents in 1825 because of the efficiencies in water transportation (Levanen 2000). Commerce grew at an amazing rate each year. As Hatcher (1945, 181) notes, "Detroit, as both a way station and an embarkation point for the lands farther west, felt the stirrings of the continent."

During these early European settlement years, settlers, like Native Americans before them, had a close relationship to the Detroit River through "ribbon farms" that allowed each property owner access to the riverfront and the freshwater so necessary for human, wildlife, and plant survival. But this close human relationship with the river began to diminish as Detroit developed into a leading center of commerce and trade. In fact, the Detroit River became so busy with ship traffic that it was declared a public highway by act of Congress on December 3, 1819.

Increased commercial activity and trade in Detroit soon led to industrial development. Holli (1976) noted that Detroit reached a high plateau of commercial development during 1850–70 and concluded that

TONY SPINA COLLECTION, WALTER P. REUTHER LIBRARY, WAYNE STATE UNIVERSITY

FIGURE 2. Detroit's riverfront in 1950 when it was the fifth largest city in the United States with a population of nearly 1.9 million.

Detroit's primary processing industries and trade-serving manufactures during this era were the building blocks and provided the knowledge for a factory town that would eventually mass-produce automobiles. By the 1890s, Detroit had earned a solid national reputation as a center of railroad car manufacturing, shipbuilding, cigar making, and stove production. In addition, more passenger trade went out of Detroit in the 1890s than anywhere in the world.

Surrounded by a plethora of untapped natural resources and afforded competitive advantage through water and rail transportation, Detroit turned iron from Lake Superior's Mesabi Range into stoves and railcars, and eventually cars by the millions (Martelle 2012). Indeed, by 1914 Detroit was making half the country's cars. This vibrant industrial manufacturing and commercial hub attracted so many entrepreneurs, labor organizers, European immigrants, and African Americans from the South that it became the fourth largest city in the United States in 1929. By the middle of the twentieth century one in six American jobs were connected to the automobile industry, and the Motor City was its epicenter (Martelle 2012). It should be no surprise that Detroit reached the apex of its population growth in 1950 with nearly 1.9 million people (figure 2).

Through Detroit's human population growth and industrial expansion, the Detroit River became one of the most polluted rivers in the United States, and Detroit residents further lost connection to their river. The Detroit River was clearly perceived as a working river that supported commerce and technological progress. Like many other large North American cities, the Motor City made the Detroit River its back door, with businesses facing inland and away from the river (Hartig and Wallace 2015). Compounding the problem, Detroit became indifferent to the water pollution that was perceived as just part of the cost of doing business (Hartig 2010).

Since the 1960s, Detroit has experienced considerable loss of population and industry, rising unemployment, increased cost of living, decreased access to city services, and increased crime. To many, it became the poster child of the Rust Belt. In total, Detroit has experienced a 60 percent loss in population and considerable losses in manufacturing and industrial jobs since 1960. During this era, it became a city more often characterized by hardship than success. This industrial decline, population emigration, loss of jobs, and concomitant other socioeconomic problems culminated in 2013 when Detroit became the largest city in the United States to ever go through bankruptcy.

This book is not another book about the rise and fall of Detroit, but a story of how Detroit is turning to the Detroit River and embracing it through a new waterfront porch to help revitalize the city and region, and to help foster a more sustainable future. It is a story of one of the largest, by scale, urban waterfront redevelopment projects in the United States that will give hope and will help provide evidence that Detroit and its metropolitan region have a bright future. Also shared in the end will be the important lessons learned about how it is being done to encourage more urban conservation and sustainability initiatives throughout the world, and to inspire and recruit the next generation of conservationists and sustainability entrepreneurs from urban areas because that is now where most people on our planet live.

CHAPTER 1

Detroit's History in Addressing Paradigm Shifts

History is sometimes described as our collective memory. More formally is has been described as the branch of knowledge dealing with past events. If we are ignorant of history or have a defective collective memory, then we do not have sufficient knowledge to guide effective public action. That is undoubtedly why the philosopher and novelist George Santayana developed the following famous quote: "Those who cannot remember the past are condemned to repeat it."

Detroit has a long and rich history, dating back to Native Americans and its founding in 1701. To better understand the historical changes that have taken place in and along the Detroit River, the changes in human relationship with it, and the current desire to reconnect to it, this chapter will review Detroit's history and role in addressing paradigm shifts.

History has taught us that periodically there is a significant change in thinking that results in a completely changed view or outlook. Certain agents of change bring about these new ways of thinking or doing things, often described as revolutions or transformations.

Paradigm Shifts

Thomas Kuhn, a well-known physicist, philosopher, and historian of science, described and popularized this concept of significant changes in thinking that result in completely changed views or outlooks and called them "paradigm shifts." Kuhn (1962) argued that scientific advancement is not evolutionary, but rather should be viewed as periods of stable growth punctuated by revisionary revolutions. N. Wade, in a review of Kuhn's seminal book, further described the advancement of science as a "series of peaceful interludes punctuated by intellectually violent revolutions," and in those revolutions "one conceptual world view is replaced by another" (1977, 144). Paradigm shifts are therefore revolutions, transformations, or even metamorphoses. They do not just happen, but are driven by agents of change. First introduced to explain how science changes over time, paradigm shifts are now used to explain changes in business, social movements, and beyond.

For example, the invention of the printing press by Johann Gutenberg in the 1440s brought about a paradigm shift that allowed books to be readily available to all people. Similarly, personal computers and the Internet in recent years have brought about a paradigm shift in both personal and business environments.

Metropolitan Detroit has gone through a number of these paradigm shifts. Change is always difficult. But metropolitan Detroit has a long history of adapting well to paradigm shifts and meeting the needs of the region and indeed the world. Presented below are the major paradigm shifts that have affected metropolitan Detroit, insights into how metropolitan Detroit has responded, some of the unintended consequences, and current information on how it is responding to the latest sustainability paradigm shift.

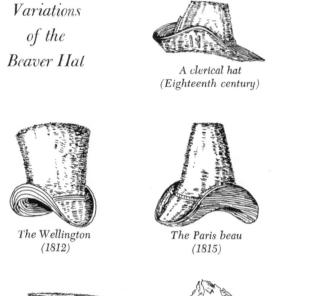

Variations of the Beaver Hat

A clerical hat
(Eighteenth century)

The continental
cocked hat
(1776)

The Wellington
(1812)

The Paris beau
(1815)

The D'orsay
(1820)

The regent
(1825)

FIGURE 3. European fashion during the seventeenth, eighteenth, and nineteenth centuries demanded fur hats made of beaver pelts.

The Fur Trade: The First Paradigm Shift

During the late 1600s and early 1700s beaver-pelt hats had become quite the rage in Europe (figure 3). Most French aristocrats and the more affluent members of the middle class wore fur hats. As these hats grew in popularity, demand for European beaver pelts grew. Beaver, once as common in the Old World as the New, had been eradicated everywhere in Europe except for eastern Russia and the steep valleys of the Pyrenees, a region far too small to supply the fashion needs of a prosperous continent (D. Muir 2000). As beaver supplies in Europe were depleted to meet this growing mercantile attraction, explorers began to look at North America as a potential source of beaver. The Great Lakes Basin, including Michigan and the Detroit River watershed, had millions of beaver. A paradigm shift had occurred, driven by a relentless European demand for beaver-pelt hats.

One could say that Detroit was created in response to the first paradigm shift of European demand for hats made from beaver pelts. Antoine de la Mothe Cadillac founded Detroit in 1701 to establish a military presence at the "narrows of the river" to control water traffic and win a fur trade monopoly. This was important to both advance the French fur trade and protect it from the English and Iroquois (Johnson 1919). Not only did Detroit become a major center for collecting and exporting furs, it became a major center for processing of furs.

It is estimated that there were about ten million beaver in North America when the Europeans arrived (Dunbar and May 1995). Europeans exported fifty thousand skins annually until, by 1800, numbers of beaver were substantially reduced and nearly extirpated east of the Mississippi. It was recorded that during the height of beaver exploitation during the eighteenth and nineteenth centuries, hundreds of thousands of beaver skins were exported to Europe from North America annually (Johnson 1919). D. Muir (2000) noted that Native Americans did not kill beaver in a conscious decision to extirpate them or deplete the population; they were simply swept up by economic forces that were deemed irresistible.

By the late 1830s the fur trade in Detroit began to decline (Johnson 1919). Detroit merchants no longer depended on furs. Commerce, agriculture, and lumbering became the basis of the next economy. The last time beaver was reported in the Detroit River was 1877 (Johnson 1919). Ceaseless slaughter led to nearly wiping out the beavers in the United States east of the Mississippi River by 1930.

Shipbuilding: The Second Paradigm Shift

During the late 1700s and 1800s Detroit had become a major center of trade and commerce. Detroit, as both a way station and an embarkation point for the lands farther west, felt the tremendous stirrings of the continent (Hatcher 1945).

Detroit was once again in the midst of a paradigm shift initiated by settlement of the west. There was an immediate and pressing demand for transportation of passengers and freight. The Detroit metropolitan area met this transportation demand by becoming one of the greatest shipbuilding ports in the United States. Detroit's strategic location in the Great Lakes, its position as a center of commerce, and the availability of essential resources contributed to it becoming a great shipbuilding port.

Detroit's first shipyard was constructed by the British in 1760 to produce armed naval vessels and commercial sailing craft. Levanen (2000, 9) provides the following account of the history of shipbuilding in Detroit:

> Hundreds of ships were built along the waterfront. In 1907, twenty-one of the largest ships sailing the lakes were launched in Detroit. The waterfront was dotted with shipbuilding rigs, launching docks, and drydocks . . . One third of all marine engines built in the United States from 1897 to 1920 were built in Detroit. Some of these famous builders were Riverside Iron Works, located at the foot of Chene Street, Frontier Iron Works, situated near Belle Isle, and the Dry Dock Engineering Works, located at the foot of Orleans Street.

It was a logical extension that Detroit would later become a major center for production of paint varnish, steam and gasoline engines, metal pipes and parts, and over one hundred other marine parts. In fact, during the 1890s more ships were built in the Detroit area along the Detroit River than in any other city in America (figure 4).

FARMER 1890

FIGURE 4. Dry docks and repair yard of the Detroit Dry Dock Company, Detroit, Michigan, circa 1884.

Shipbuilding was also significant along the lower end of the Detroit River. From 1801 to 1960 at least 655 ships were built at yards and locations from the lower Rouge River downstream to the mouth of the Detroit River. Detroit's significance as a shipbuilding center and transportation corridor was manifested by U.S. Congress in 1819, when the Detroit River was proclaimed a public highway. In addition, more passenger trade went out of Detroit than anywhere in the world during the 1890s. Shipbuilding provided jobs and supported families locally, but it also had a significant impact on our region, the nation, and the world. Over the years these ships would help further billions of dollars of commerce and trade.

One of the unintended consequences of shipping was spills that caused short-term pollution of our waterways. In more recent years, numerous invasive aquatic species have been introduced into the Great Lakes from the discharge of ballast water from ships entering the Great Lakes from overseas. Two good examples are zebra and quagga mussels that caused dramatic changes in the Great Lakes food web and millions of dollars in increased treatment costs for municipal water intakes and other industries that draw surface water for operations.

Automobile Manufacturing: The Third Paradigm Shift

Metropolitan Detroit's expertise in building steam engines for ships and practical experience in manufacturing coaches and carriages positioned it well for addressing the automotive paradigm shift. This technological capacity and practical experience enabled Henry Ford, Ransom Olds, and other entrepreneurial automakers to put together their first models with off-the-shelf parts.

Detroit's first car company started in 1899. However, it did not take long for automobile manufacturing to take off. Henry Ford believed that cars should be affordable to everyone (figure 5). To help achieve that goal, he created more efficient manufacturing systems, including assembly lines. By 1913 the industry grew to the point where there were forty-three different automobile companies operating in the Detroit area. In 1914, Henry Ford announced that pay for an eight-hour shift in his Highland Park plant would be $8 per day (Cowles 1975). This drew a huge crowd of over ten thousand that had to be dispersed with fire hoses. Henry Ford's practice of providing loans to consumers to buy cars made the Model T affordable to the middle class. In the 1920s, General Motors further changed the industry by emphasizing car design. The company introduced new models each year, marketed different lines of cars to different income brackets, and created a modern decentralized system of management.

Automobile manufacturing would soon dominate the economy of the Detroit area. In 1904, 3.8 percent of Detroit's 60,554 industrial employees were employed in the automobile industry. In 1919, 45 percent of Detroit's 308,520 industrial employees were employed in the automobile industry

FIGURE 5. Henry Ford with the ten-millionth Model T and the 1896 Quadricycle, 1924.

(Holli 1976). Detroit became the Motor City and one of the largest industrial manufacturing centers in the world.

Like many major urban areas throughout the United States, people began moving away from Detroit beginning in the 1950s seeking suburban areas with more space and within driving distance to their workplace as the suburbs developed. Personal automobiles and cheap fuel made this possible. In addition, federal tax subsidies for home mortgage interest and property taxes, as well as infrastructure financing policies, all supported new growth outside existing cities.

This outward migration of people from Detroit to the suburbs resulted in an increase in the amount of urban land developed and a decrease in density (i.e., people per unit of area) due to the automobile. This pattern of people moving out of the city to the surrounding suburbs created a longer commute. The greater number of people driving to work every morning created an environmental stressor with additional road construction, air pollution, urban runoff, and the overuse of natural resources, such as petroleum. Clearly, an unintended consequence of the automobile, under the good intention of expanding personal freedom to travel, was urban sprawl.

Other environmental impacts have included air pollution and water pollution that both have gotten progressively better with national (e.g., Clean Air Act of 1970; Clean Water Act of 1972) and state regulations, and technological advances. Further, the decentralization of the automobile industry and the emigration of people, downsizing, and disinvestment in Detroit all had substantial impacts on the economic, social, and environmental health of the city.

Arsenal of Democracy: The Fourth Paradigm Shift

Following the Japanese attack on Pearl Harbor in 1941, the United States plunged into the Second World War. President Franklin D. Roosevelt had recognized the need to help supply Europe with the implements of war and implored Americans to stand up as the "arsenal of democracy" as though it was their own war. The president called on the nation to unite with swift cooperation in producing vast shipments of weaponry to aid Europe. Detroit once again responded to a paradigm shift by, this time, redeploying its vast industrial capacity to play a critical role in the ultimate Allied victory in 1945.

Metropolitan Detroit factories halted the production of automobiles for civilian use and began rapidly producing jeeps, M-5 tanks, and B-24 bombers until the end of the war (Davis 2007). By the summer of 1944, Ford Motor Company's Willow Run plant manufactured one B-24 Liberator Bomber an hour. Ford Motor Company's Rouge Plant was converted into a tank arsenal (figure 6). In total, metropolitan Detroit

COURTESY OF THE NATIONAL AUTOMOTIVE HISTORY COLLECTION, DETROIT PUBLIC LIBRARY

FIGURE 6. Tanks roll off the assembly line at the Detroit Arsenal, Warren, Michigan, circa mid-1940s.

companies received contracts worth about $14 billion or 10 percent of all U.S. military output in 1943. By 1944 metropolitan Detroit was the leading supplier of military goods in the United States. Metropolitan Detroit responded to the "arsenal of democracy" paradigm shift by producing about $29 billion of military output during 1942–45. Approximately 610,000 people in metropolitan Detroit were employed in this military production that ranged from ball bearings to bombers and trucks to tanks. Metropolitan Detroit's manufacturing capability and technical expertise were key factors in addressing this paradigm shift and helping meet the military needs of both the United States and Europe.

But winning the war would also have unintended consequences. The country's sole focus was winning the war. There were no major environmental regulations, and it was way before the Clean Water Act of

1972. During a very cold January 1948, the Detroit River was substantially covered with ice. That meant that there were only a few pockets of open water where migrating waterfowl could stop, rest, and feed. The Detroit River is well known both as a major migration corridor for twenty-nine species of waterfowl and for over three hundred thousand diving ducks that stop each year to feed on wild celery.

During 1946–48, the U.S. Department of Health, Education, and Welfare (1962) estimated that approximately 5.93 million gallons of oil and other petroleum products were being discharged into the Rouge and Detroit rivers each year. To put this in perspective, this volume of oil being discharged was enough to virtually pollute the entire western basin of Lake Erie, including all Michigan, Ohio, and Ontario waters (Hartig 2010). That meant that the few remaining pockets of open water on the Detroit River were covered with oil and that instead of landing in water, the waterfowl, looking for places to rest and feed, landed in the oil. A few days later eleven thousand waterfowl died from that oil pollution

FIGURE 7. Michigan conservation officer with oil-soaked ducks from the Detroit River that had died from oil pollution, 1948.

(Cowles 1975) (figure 7). Angry sportsmen from communities along the lower Detroit River collected the oil-soaked carcasses of ducks and geese, put them in their pickup trucks, drove them to Michigan Capitol in Lansing, threw them on to the capitol lawn and sidewalk in protest, and held a press conference in opposition to the oil pollution (Hartig 2010). This single event is now credited with starting the industrial pollution control program of Michigan (Cowles 1975).

Sustainability: The Most Recent Paradigm Shift

In the early days of Detroit, the interests of commerce and industry were clearly put in front of the interests of the environment. Back then, the primary role of business in society was to make money, and people didn't think much about the environment. Therefore, the riverfront was developed to support industry and commerce. Again, Detroit was an industrial town that put free market economics first.

That thinking changed in the 1980s when the concept of sustainable development was popularized and endorsed by business and legitimized through the work of the World Commission on Environment and Development and its book *Our Common Future* (Bruntland 1987). Proponents, many from the business community, argued compellingly that development must meet the needs of the present generation without compromising the ability of future generations to meet their own needs. The need was for environmentally and socially sustainable economic development. This concept is often presented as a Venn diagram that depicts sustainability as a balance among the three pillars of civilization: economy, environment, and society (figure 8). To help communicate the concept and to build broad-based support for its use, the business community described it as balanced and continuous social, economic, and environmental progress. No single pillar would receive greater weight in decision making than the others.

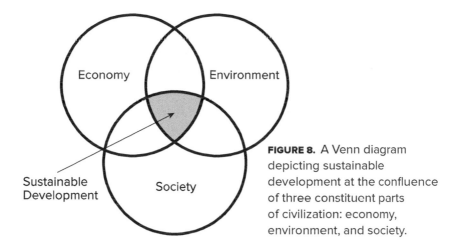

FIGURE 8. A Venn diagram depicting sustainable development at the confluence of three constituent parts of civilization: economy, environment, and society.

The business sector went on to further explain and champion sustainable development with use of the phrase "triple bottom line." Everyone had heard of the traditional measure of corporate profit—the bottom line of the profit and loss account. However, proponents of sustainable development, including key business thinkers, were advocating for two other equal bottom lines. These included a company's "people account," a measure of how socially responsible it has been throughout its operations, and a company's "planet account," a measure of how environmentally responsible it has been. The triple bottom line thus consists of the three "Ps": profit, people, and planet. It aims to measure the financial, social, and environmental performance of a business over a period of time. Only a company that produces a triple bottom line is taking account of the full cost involved in doing business and avoiding unintended consequences.

During the 1970s and early 1980s many environmental issues were characterized by adversarial relationships that polarized environment and development. Much of the argument centered on either protecting the environment or furthering development. The concept of sustainable development brought the free enterprise system together with the environmental movement to see that a healthy economy and a healthy community require a healthy environment.

Across the world, governments, corporations, nongovernmental organizations, and academic institutions were setting up roundtable discussions and work groups to find new ways and means to balance economic, social, and environmental goals toward the long-term need of sustainable development. Metropolitan Detroit businesses became early leaders of the sustainability movement (table 1). They recognized that to ensure long-term competitive advantage they needed to prevent pollution and achieve environmentally sustainable economic development and pay more attention to attracting and retaining the next generation of employees.

As you can imagine, metropolitan Detroit has been much concerned about the number of graduates that leave the area, never to return. Many move to other areas that provide greater opportunities and a higher quality of life. Metropolitan Detroit's image of being part of the Rust Belt and being polluted contributed to the perception of low quality of life. Metropolitan Detroit businesses recognized this problem and have invested heavily in sustainability to achieve competitive business advantage, to improve the environment in the place they call home, and to attract and retain the next generation of employees.

Detroit even hosted the 1999 National Town Hall Meeting for the President's Council on Sustainable Development on May 2–5, at its Cobo Convention Center. More than three thousand people attended this national gathering that brought stakeholders together representing economy, society, and environment to find common ground and to explore ways and means of implementing sustainable development in the different sectors. This helped put Detroit on the map for leadership on sustainable development and inspired many local organizations and institutions to accelerate advancing the sustainability agenda.

Metropolitan Detroit is still in the early stages of responding to the sustainability paradigm shift, with businesses providing key leadership through operational programs like ISO 14000, ISO 9000, Design for Environment, Responsible Care, Full Cost Accounting and others.

TABLE 1. Examples of Major Metropolitan Detroit Corporations That Were Early Leaders in the Sustainability Paradigm Shift

CORPORATION (HEADQUARTERS OR PLANT LOCATION)	
PRODUCTS MANUFACTURED	CORPORATE COMMITMENT TO SUSTAINABILITY
Ford Motor Company (Dearborn, Michigan)	
One-hundred-year history of automobile manufacturing	Ford has a strong commitment to sustainable development, including implementing a "Blueprint for Sustainability" across the company.
General Motors Corporation (Detroit, Michigan)	
The world's third largest automaker and the industry sales leader in the U.S. in 2016	Environmental stewardship and sustainability are part of the General Motors business model and core to their operations, including producing an annual "Sustainability Report."
Fiat Chrysler Automobiles (FCA) (North American headquarters in Auburn Hills, Michigan)	
Designs, engineers, manufactures, and sells passenger cars, light commercial vehicles, components, and production systems worldwide	FCA has a strong commitment to sustainable development, including reporting on performance indicators through its annual "Sustainability Report."
DTE Energy (Detroit, Michigan)	
One of the largest electric utilities in Michigan, providing electricity to 2.2 million people in southeast Michigan	DTE Energy is dedicated to sustainable development as a way of doing business, including minimizing their ecological footprint of today and developing sustainable energy resources for tomorrow. DTE is Michigan's largest investor in and producer of renewable energy.
Consumers Energy	
An integrated energy company that provides natural gas and electricity to 6.7 million Michigan residents	Consumers Energy meets the needs of its customers while continuing to protect the natural resources. In 2016, ranked in the top 6 percent among global utilities for sustainable environmental, social, and economic practices.
BASF Corporation (plant in Wyandotte, Michigan)	

International chemical company with a diverse product mix including chemicals, polymers, automotive and industrial coatings, colorants, and agricultural products	BASF has a strong commitment to sustainable development through Responsible Care initiatives and through the work of a Sustainability Council that integrates sustainability into organizational and management systems.
Masco Corporation (Livonia, Michigan)	
One of the world's largest manufacturers of brand-name products for the home improvement and new home construction markets	Masco has a strong commitment to developing innovative and environmentally friendly products, reducing energy usage, and conducting business that protects the environment. It uses Global Reporting Initiative Guidelines to measure sustainability practices, outcomes, and activities.
Eastman (plant in Trenton, Michigan)	
A global chemical company that produces a broad range of advanced materials, additives and functional products, specialty chemicals, and fibers that are found in products people use every day	Eastman has a strong commitment to sustainable development through the American Chemistry Council's Responsible Care Program and produces an annual sustainability progress report.
Visteon Corporation (Van Buren, Michigan)	
A global technology company that designs, engineers, and manufactures innovative cockpit electronics products and connected car solutions for most of the world's major vehicle manufacturers	Visteon is committed to corporate sustainability and citizenship. It produces an annual "Sustainability Report" that documents initiatives, practices, and achievements related to ethics and governance, diversity, environment, health and safety, and community involvement.
Federal-Mogul Corporation (Southfield, Michigan)	
An innovative and diversified global supplier of quality products, trusted brands, and creative solutions to manufacturers of automotive, light commercial, heavy-duty, and off-highway vehicles, as well as in power generation, aerospace, marine, rail, and industrial	Federal-Mogul is committed to enabling a healthier and more productive world. It produces a "Sustainability Report" that measures how the corporation supports people through active community engagement, protects the environment by operating in a sustainable manner, and develops innovative, advanced products in a fashion that enables increased efficiency, improved fuel consumption, and a reduction in emissions.
U.S. Steel (USS) (Ecorse, Michigan)	

An integrated steel producer that manufactures a wide range of value-added steel sheet and tubular products for the automotive, appliance, container, industrial machinery, construction, and oil and gas industries	USS is committed to principles of sustainable development in manufacturing innovative products that meet society's needs; this commitment is aimed at improving the quality of life for everyone now and for generations to come. (The steel industry's commitment to sustainability has transformed steel into the world's most recycled material.)
Praxair (Detroit and River Rouge, Michigan)	
An industrial gas company that develops technologies, products, and services that help to sustain and protect our planet	Praxair is committed to the principles of sustainable development and works to reduce their environmental footprint while helping customers worldwide to improve their environmental performance. It produces annual reports that measure sustainable development performance.

However, much remains to be done within all societal sectors and organizations to operationalize sustainability in management programs and day-to-day operations. But, as noted above, Detroit has historically demonstrated ingenuity, creativity, and technological excellence in meeting the needs of our region, nation, and world.

Detroit is a relatively large city with 139 square miles, enough land to put the cities of Boston, Massachusetts, Buffalo, New York, Harford, Connecticut, Burlington, Vermont, and Wilmington, Delaware, inside its borders. Even though Detroit has fewer people and less built environment today, it still has a lot of land. Gallagher argues that "a smaller city creates the canvas to become a better city." The experience in Youngstown, Ohio, has shown that getting smaller can translate into cost savings because fewer services have to be delivered to a smaller population (2010, 11). As Youngstown mayor Jay Williams has said: "A city getting smaller may gain flexibility to become more innovative. New ideas and approaches can be tested on a more manageable scale with quicker results" (Gallagher 2010, 12).

That is precisely what Detroit Future City is doing through the implementation of an ambitious, but attainable, blueprint for transforming Detroit from a state of population loss and excessive vacancy into a model for the reinvention of postindustrial American cities. Probably the best way to describe Detroit Future City is as a model by which the city is being reimagined, determining where and how resources should be concentrated and invested to make the city move livable, attractive, and sustainable. At a practical level this means that there will be places in Detroit that will receive less attention.

A clear vision is supported by measurable goals. For example, Detroit Future City (2012) believes that by 2030 Detroit should:

- have a stabilized population of six hundred thousand to eight hundred thousand residents and to remain one of the largest top twenty cities in the United States;
- have fifty jobs for every one hundred city residents, instead of twenty-seven private-sector jobs for every one hundred Detroiters reported in 2012;
- have an integrated regional public transportation system for the metropolitan region;
- have become a world leader in developing landscape as twenty-first-century infrastructure to transform vacant land areas into community assets that remediate contaminated land, manage stormwater and highway runoff, and create passive recreational amenities to improve human health and elevate adjacent land values;
- be enhanced and sustained by a broad-based and ongoing civic stewardship framework of leadership drawn from among philanthropists, businesses, residents, faith institutions, major civic and cultural institutions, and a range of regional and national supporters; and
- have become a city for all, with an enhanced range of choices for

all residents, especially those who have stayed through the hardest times.

Detroit Future City is now working with partners to implement its blueprint through twelve imperative actions:

- reenergizing Detroit's economy to increase job opportunities for Detroiters within the city and strengthen the tax base
- supporting current residents and attracting new residents
- utilizing innovative approaches to transform vacant land in ways that increase value and productivity, and promote long-term sustainability
- using open space to improve the health of all Detroit's residents
- promoting a range of sustainable residential densities
- sizing the networks for a smaller population, making them more efficient, more affordable, and better performing
- realigning city systems in ways that promote areas of economic potential, encourage thriving communities, and improve environmental and human health conditions
- ensuring strategic and coordinated use of land
- promoting stewardship for all areas of the city by implementing short- and long-term strategies
- providing residents with meaningful ways to make change in their communities and the city at large
- pursuing a collaborative regional agenda that recognizes Detroit's strengths and our region's shared destiny
- ensuring all citizens are dedicated to implementing the framework for their future.

There is no doubt that the work of Detroit Future City is having an impact in Detroit becoming a more sustainable city.

In 2017 Detroit mayor Mike Duggan established an Office of

Sustainability to guide the city of Detroit's efforts to strengthen the economic, social, and environmental well-being of the city's residents, neighborhoods, and businesses. This made sustainability a priority within the administration. Current priorities are to improve green infrastructure in Detroit, clean up air quality, and promote urban farming, among other initiatives.

Based on historical precedent, technological advantage, ingenuity, and work ethic, metropolitan Detroit can be a leader in the sustainability paradigm shift through urban agriculture, urban food distribution, green infrastructure, green architecture, brownfield cleanup and re-development, greenways, automobile technology, affordable housing, and innovative and alternative energy. Indeed, there are already many promising signs (table 2).

Concluding Remarks

Detroit was the epicenter of the fur trade era, an unparalleled leader of shipbuilding for one hundred years, the Silicon Valley of the industrial age, and the unquestioned leader of the arsenal of democracy. This unique history shows that Detroit is a city of innovation, creativity, resilience, and leadership in responding to paradigm shifts. Detroit now has the ability to be a critical leader of sustainable redevelopment, pivoting, as it has done at each previous paradigm shift, to redefine itself and lead the nation and world down a more sustainable path.

One of the major challenges for large old cities like Detroit is to transform their industry-dominated waterfronts into more sustainable ones that equally promote a healthy and vibrant economy, environment, and society. History has shown that waterfronts should not be developed for a single purpose, as was done in many large North American cities, and that a mix of uses must be pursued that supports industry and commerce, improves the environment, and provides benefits that enhance quality of

TABLE 2. Selected Examples of How Detroit Is Demonstrating Leadership in Sustainable Development

Urban Agriculture	• In 2016, Detroit had over 1,400 community, backyard, church, and school gardens and farms, producing over 170 tons of organic produce.
	• In 2016, the Michigan Urban Farming Initiative debuted America's first sustainable urban "agrihood," an alternative neighborhood growth model in Detroit's lower North End that positions agriculture as the centerpiece of a mixed-use urban development.
	• The Michigan State University Center for Urban Food Systems has been established in Detroit to facilitate best practices for food and nonfood plant production and a variety of related community support activities.
	• Hantz Farms is creating the largest urban tree farm in the United States on the east side of Detroit in support of making neighborhoods more livable.
Urban Food Distribution	• Eastern Market is one of the largest year-round public markets in the United States and has been a staple of urban activity and commerce for more than one hundred years; it draws more than forty thousand visitors weekly, providing fresh food options to residents and visitors and providing opportunities for entrepreneurs and small businesses.
	• Capuchin Soup Kitchen's Earthworks Urban Farm is committed to creating a food system for all, including growing food, "healthy corner stores," a Field of Our Dreams mobile produce truck, support for sales of produce at local health clinics, donations to soup kitchens, and neighborhood farmers' markets.
	• Detroit businesses, like Avalon International Breads, support Detroit's Garden Resource Program that promotes family, community, school, and market gardens that foster urban agriculture within a thriving local food system.
Green Architecture	• A green building culture is emerging in Detroit.
	• Although the Detroit market ranked twenty-fifth in the Green Building Adoption Index, it is a standout when it comes to larger construction.
	• In Dearborn, Ford Motor Company spent $2 billion on transforming the historic Rouge Plant from a twentieth-century icon of automobile manufacturing to a twenty-first-century model of sustainable manufacturing; it has one of the largest green roofs in the world.

Green Infrastructure	• Since 1989, Greening of Detroit has planted nearly one hundred thousand trees in Detroit as part of enhancing green infrastructure (i.e., a network of planned and managed green spaces that work together to benefit a community's social, economic, and environmental health).
	• Southeast Michigan Council of Governments and the Detroit Water and Sewerage Department are implementing a green infrastructure vision and plan.
	• Detroit Future City recommended green infrastructure as a priority for addressing urban stormwater problems, and the city of Detroit is implementing projects.
	• In the Rouge River watershed, the Alliance of Rouge Communities is championing green infrastructure to address stormwater issues.
Brownfield Cleanup and Redevelopment	• Brownfield cleanup at the former Uniroyal Tire Plant site along the Detroit River was completed at a cost of nearly $33.5 million to become part of the Detroit RiverWalk with mixed-use redevelopment along Jefferson Avenue.
	• A former industrial brownfield site along the Detroit River was cleaned up as part of the thirty-one-acre Milliken State Park in Detroit.
	• In Trenton, a forty-four-acre brownfield was cleaned up and restored to become the gateway to the Detroit River International Wildlife Refuge.
	• In Wyandotte, BASF helped convert an eighty-four-acre brownfield into a nine-hole golf course, twenty-five-acre waterfront park, boardwalk, and world-class rowing facility.
	• BASF restored the 1,200-acre Fighting Island from a former brine disposal area into a wildlife sanctuary that has received Wildlife Habitat Council certification and a corporate conference and retreat center.
Greenway Trails	• Since 2001, the Community Foundation for Southeast Michigan, through its Greenways Initiative, has invested $26.5 million to help communities build greenway trails, leveraging an additional $90 million in public and private funding.
	• Detroit Greenways Coalition works to promote and build a network of greenways and bike lanes that will connect people and places, improve the quality of life, beautify neighborhoods, and stimulate neighborhood-level economic development in Detroit; it is championing a Joe Louis Greenway that is a twenty-six-mile nonmotorized pathway encircling the city of Detroit and running through the cities of Hamtramck, Highland Park, and Dearborn.

Greenway Trails (*continued*)	▪ A bike-sharing program makes bicycles available twenty-four hours a day, every day of the year (except during severe weather) through MoGo, a program run by the nonprofit Detroit Bike Share, which is affiliated with the Downtown Detroit Partnership; some 430 bikes are spread across forty-three stations located in ten neighborhoods around the city.
Automobile Technology	▪ Automobile manufacturers have been leaders in hybrids and plug-in hybrids and are collaborating to produce autonomous vehicles and hydrogen-powered electric vehicles and the infrastructure to support them.
	▪ Ford Motor Company is locating its autonomous vehicle and electric vehicle business and strategy teams, including Team Edison in Detroit's Corktown neighborhood.
Affordable Housing	▪ Billionaire developer Steven Ross and the New York–based Ford Foundation have teamed up with the Platform LLC to invest $27.5 million in housing in Detroit neighborhoods.
	▪ The city of Detroit works with developers on a project-by-project basis with the goal of making at least 20 percent of units in newly built developments affordable for low-income people.
	▪ Habitat for Humanity Detroit (Habitat Detroit) is a nonprofit housing ministry that provides low-income, working families the opportunity to purchase modest, affordable housing in which to raise their families.
	▪ The Michigan Suburbs Alliance is piloting Green Anchors, an innovative program that takes a holistic approach to affordable housing, green buildings, and community engagement.
	▪ Detroit is experimenting with a neighborhood of "tiny houses" (i.e., four hundred square feet) for homeless and special needs persons.
Innovative and Alternative Energy	▪ NextEnergy is a nonprofit organization established in 2002 and one of the nation's leading accelerators of advanced energy and transportation technologies, businesses, and industries; it has helped attract more than $1.5 billion of new investment, including programs in excess of $160 million in which NextEnergy has directly participated.
	▪ ZeroBase is a leading innovator in hybrid power systems located in Ferndale, Michigan.

Innovative and Alternative Energy (*continued*)	• DTE Energy has committed to a broad sustainability initiative that will reduce the company's carbon emissions by more than 80 percent by 2050 through a fundamental transformation of power generation to more renewable energy and natural gas–fired power plants.
	• Ryter Cooperative Industries of Sterling Heights focuses on helping community-based organizations integrate green energy and energy efficiency; its highest-profile project thus far is building a three-kilowatt solar energy station at D-Town Farms, a seven-acre urban farm located at Rouge Park in northwest Detroit.
Climate Change	• In 2017 Detroit mayor Mike Duggan joined 350 other mayors to agree to the principles of the Paris Climate Accord.
	• A Detroit Climate Action Plan was released in 2017 by a coalition of twenty-six businesses, environmental and community groups, and universities to address climate change, public health, and environmental justice issues.

life and contribute to a vibrant community. Indeed, this is one area that can reap enormous benefits. And that is precisely what Detroit is now doing, transforming its postindustrial riverfront into a new waterfront porch that improves the economy, enhances the society by improving quality of life and celebrating its rich history and culture, and protects the environment. But first we need a better understanding of Detroit's history in waterfront development, including how and why its waterfront evolved into such an underutilized and underappreciated state.

CHAPTER 2

Historical Changes in the Riverfront

When thinking about all the paradigm shifts that Detroit has gone through and often led, it should be no surprise that the shoreline of the Detroit River has gone through many anthropogenic changes. This chapter will review the changes in the shoreline of the Detroit River from the Native American era through right before the creation of the Detroit RiverFront Conservancy when the riverfront was dominated by dilapidated and abandoned buildings, and by much underutilized and undervalued riverfront land, characteristic of the Rust Belt.

Native American Era

Native Americans lived along the Detroit River for over a millennium before Europeans came to the region (table 3). Native Americans called this area *Wawiiatanong*, which means "the place on the curve or bend" and refers to the location of the earliest historical village of Algonquins living along the river (Cornell 2003). The reason these Native Americans occupied this region for such a long time was the incredible natural resource base and access to water as an efficient transportation route. The Native Americans of *Wawiiatanong* were subsisting on a varied diet of large game, small game, plant products, and fish. Historical research has shown that the shoreline was dominated by wetlands and floodplains (Cornell 2003). The floodplains with rich soils supported native agriculture, and the shallow inlets and embayments provided ideal habitat for wild rice (an important food stuff).

Wawiiatanong was clearly the heart of Native American commerce and subsistence. Native peoples used dugout and bark canoes to fish for lake sturgeon, channel catfish, suckers, northern pike, largemouth and smallmouth bass, perch, and walleye in the rapids and backwaters, and to travel to seasonal encampments (Cornell 2003). The numerous adjacent marshes were rich in waterfowl and their eggs and in turtles. Muskrat were an important food of Native Americans that could easily be hunted in the river, tributary creeks, and marshes. The lands surrounding *Wawiiatanong* were also home to beaver that built networks of beaver dams that provided a system of crossings and walkways for native hunters in the lowland areas. These wetlands also attracted deer that were highly valued as food and as a source of hides for indigenous peoples.

Based on the best available historical research of the Native American era and earliest maps, the river shoreline consisted of coastal wetlands up to a mile wide along both sides of the river. Vegetation types included submerged marsh, emergent marsh, wet meadow and shrub swamp, swamp forest, and lake-plain prairie. Suffice it to say that the Detroit River shoreline during this era was made up of highly diverse wetland and riparian habitats that both attracted and sustained Native Americans. Upon his arrival in 1701, Cadillac described the Detroit River shoreline in this way (Farmer 1890, 11): "Its borders are so many prairies (what we think of as marshes) and freshness of the beautiful waters keep the banks always green." Native Americans clearly viewed themselves as the inheritors of a bounty provided for them as a part of creation (Cornell 2003). Oral traditions of the early Algonquins clearly state that the plants, animals, and waters were gifts to "the People" from the Creator and that Native Americans were responsible for sustaining them (Cornell 2003). Their belief was that the plants and animals made life possible for native peoples. Further, they ritually appeased the land and living things that had to die so their families could survive.

The river was also a source of commerce and news from distant villages. Goods were brought to *Wawiiatanong* to be traded or given to relatives as gifts (Cornell 2003). The river also facilitated communication among different clans and families that journeyed to *Wawiiatanong* to attend feasts and ceremonies. All these activities, from hunting to gathering to fishing to feasting to celebrating, created a sense of place on the banks of the river at *Wawiiatanong*.

European Settlement and the Fur Trade

Antoine de la Mothe Cadillac founded Detroit in 1701 as a French trading post and garrison to expand trade and commerce (Binelli 2013). Cadillac's vision was for a strong French post on the Detroit River that would be a bulwark against British traders, a center of influence among Native Americans, and a key bastion in the chain of forts from Quebec to the lower Mississippi River (Hatcher 1945). His goal was to establish a military presence at the narrows of the river to control water traffic and the fur trade that moved over the river (table 3). To achieve that goal Cadillac needed to establish a full-service, self-supporting community in Detroit that provided the skills and services necessary to support the fur trade.

To help establish Detroit as a full-service community that was self-supporting, Cadillac began awarding ribbon farms soon after he arrived in 1701. These ribbon farms were long, narrow land divisions lined

TABLE 3. A Timeline of Events That Have Impacted Detroit
and Its Waterfront

DATE	EVENT
1600	Around one hundred thousand people live in five tribes in Michigan: Potawatomi, Ottawa, Ojibwa/Chippewa, Miami, and Huron. The Potawatomi, Ottawa, and Ojibwa speak similar Algonquin languages and are known as the "People of the Three Fires."
1669	French explorer Adrien Joliet and an Iroquois guide travel from the St. Mary's River down Lake Huron and camp at present-day Detroit.
1679	French explorer Robert de La Salle sails his ship, the *Griffon*, past Detroit on his way north to find a route to China.
1701	Antoine de la Mothe Cadillac establishes the first European settlement to expand trade and commerce.
1700s–mid-1800s	Fur trade flourishes in Detroit.
1760	British establish first shipyard along the Detroit River to produce naval vessels and commercial sailing craft.
1768	British construct first wharf projecting into the Detroit River.
1771	Detroit recognized as the center of the Great Lakes fur trade; Native Americans exchange pelts and furs for European goods like guns, cooking utensils, cloth, and jewelry.
1773	Detroit's population is about 1,400 with 280 houses.
1780s and 1790s	Additional wharfs were constructed, including the Merchant's and King's Wharf in 1796.
1802	First license for a ferry service across the river granted to transport livestock, produce, and people.
1805	Devastating fire destroys all two hundred wooden structures; wetlands near the foot of Woodward Avenue filled with debris from the fire and anything else found.
1806	Ferry house built on riverfront approximately fifty feet west of Woodward Avenue between Atwater and Woodbridge streets.
1812	The United States declares war against Britain over their interference with American shipping and westward expansion; it is known as the War of 1812.
1813	Captain Oliver Hazard Perry and his fleet defeat the British during the Battle of Lake Erie; the British retreat from Detroit two weeks later.

1815	Detroit incorporated as a city.
1818	First steamboat on the upper Great Lakes, called *Walk-in-the-Water*, arrives in Detroit.
1819	Detroit River becomes so busy with sailboats and steam vessels that it is declared a public highway by Congress.
1821	The fur trade is still a key export in Detroit and Michigan, but it is starting to decline due to overhunting.
1825	Completion of the Erie Canal makes Detroit a way station and embarkation point for lands further west.
1827	Detroit City Council votes to improve riverfront facilities with a sixty-foot-wide dock at the foot of Woodward Avenue.
1827	Detroit adopts its city seal and motto: *Speramus meliora; resurget cineribus*; it means "We hope for better days; it will arise from the ashes" and commemorates the Great Fire of 1805.
1828	Detroit's population is 1,517.
1830	Detroit's population is 2,222.
1832	A cholera epidemic devastates Detroit; Father Gabriel Richard cares for the stricken before he, too, dies from the disease.
1833	Detroit's first race riot occurs after Detroit's black citizens help the Blackburns, a fugitive slave couple, escape to Canada; this event starts the antislavery movement in Detroit.
1834	A second cholera epidemic kills six hundred Detroiters, nearly one-eighth of the city's population.
1836	Detroit builds its first stone-lined "Grand Sewer" (ten feet deep, more than four feet wide, and covered with arched brick) from a former creek called Savoyard Creek.
1837	Detroit's population is 9,700
1837	Michigan becomes the twenty-sixth state of the United States of America; Detroit is its first capital.
1840–1863	Underground Railroad aids forty-five thousand freedom seekers to cross the Detroit River to freedom.
1843	Ongoing border problems with the British in Canada lead to the construction of Fort Wayne; it is never attacked.
1845	Detroit's population is 13,065.
1845	William Lambert helps to operate Detroit's Underground Railroad with Sr. Joseph Ferguson, William Web, and other abolitionists.
1850	Shipping becomes Detroit's biggest industry.

1850	Detroit's population is 21,000.
1850	Bernhard Stroh founds the Stroh Brewery Company, following a family tradition he learned as a boy in Germany.
1853	George B. Russel begins building railroad cars under the business name Detroit Car and Manufacturing Company.
1854	The first rail connection between Detroit and New York City is completed.
1855	The locks at Sault Ste. Marie are finished; this enables ships to bring iron and copper ore to Detroit entirely by ship.
1860	Detroit's population is 45,619.
1861	Michigan is one of the first states to send volunteers to Washington, D.C., at the outbreak of the Civil War, many from Detroit.
1864	The first Bessemer-type steel is produced at Eureka Iron Works in Wyandotte, laying the groundwork for railroad, stove, and automobile manufacturing in Detroit.
1867	First railroad car ferry, called *Great Western*, launched.
1870	Detroit's population is 79,577; almost half the population was born in a different country.
1870	The Fifteenth Amendment is ratified, giving African Americans the right to vote; Detroit's African Americans vote for the first time.
1874– early-1900s	Construction of the Livingstone and Amherstburg Channels in the Detroit River.
1879	Detroit purchases Belle Isle, a 980-acre island on the Detroit River, from the Campau family for $200,000; it becomes a public park.
1880	Belle Isle Park designed by famous landscape architect Frederick Law Olmstead.
1880	Detroit's population is 116,342; it is a multicultural city with over forty nationalities represented.
1881	Detroit is the center of the nation's stove manufacturing industry.
1884	Belle Isle Park opens to the public; it is the largest island park in the nation.
1889	Detroit mayor Hazen Pingree proposes a plan for an extended park along Detroit's riverfront; however, it failed.
1890	Detroit's population reaches 205,876, fifteenth largest in American cities.
1890s	More ships built in Detroit than any other U.S. city.
1890s	More passenger trade goes out of Detroit than anywhere in the world.
1891–1955	Parke-Davis pharmaceutical company makes its home on the riverfront on 14.5 acres and eventually includes twenty-six buildings.

1896	Henry Ford builds his first car.
1897–1920	One-third of all marine engines built in Detroit.
1898	Bob-Lo Park is established as a recreational destination.
1899	Ransom E. Olds opens Detroit's first automobile manufacturing plant on East Jefferson near Belle Isle.
1900	Detroit is the world's largest manufacturer of heating and cooking stoves; other big industries include shipbuilding, cigars and tobacco, pharmaceuticals, beer, rail cars, and foundry and machine shop products
1900	Detroit's population is 285,704; it is the thirteenth largest city in the United States.
1900	Nearly 12 percent of Detroit's population doesn't speak English, the highest percentage in the nation.
1901	Ransom E. Olds produces the first practical American car; it can reach speeds of eighteen miles per hour and costs $650.
1905	Uniroyal Tire Plant constructed on riverfront (demolished in 1990s).
1907	Twenty-one of the largest ships sailing the Great Lakes launched in Detroit.
1910	Michigan Central Railroad Tunnel opens, transporting 243,000 railroad cars.
1911	Hudson's Department Store opens on Woodward Avenue with more than two million square feet of retail on thirty-two floors; in 1961 it was the tallest department store in the world.
1913	Henry Ford introduces the assembly line.
1913	Forty-three different automobile companies operating in the Detroit area.
1914	Henry Ford announces that pay for an eight-hour shift in his Highland Park plant would be $8 per day.
1919	Forty-five percent of Detroit's 308,520 industrial employees employed in the automobile industry.
1920–1933	Prohibition causes rum-running across the Detroit River.
1925	Walter Chrysler starts the Chrysler Corporation in Detroit; it is now headquartered in Auburn Hills, a Detroit suburb.
1930	Detroit–Windsor Tunnel opens between Detroit and Windsor.
1936	Ambassador Bridge opens between Detroit and Windsor.
1939	The Detroit Boat Club, the oldest in the nation, is formed.
1940	President Roosevelt calls on Detroit to become the "arsenal of democracy" to win World War II.

1942–1945	Metropolitan Detroit responds to the call to become the "arsenal of democracy" by producing about $29 billion of military output.
1950	Detroit's population hits 1.85 million, making it America's fourth-largest city, with 296,000 manufacturing jobs.
1956	Streetcar service ends in Detroit; the city sells its 184 streetcars to Mexico City for about $1 million.
1960	Detroit's population declines by 9 percent to about 1.6 million people.
1963	Dr. Martin Luther King Jr. and 125,000 people march down Woodward Avenue for racial equality.
1967	The Twelfth Street riot, one of the largest in U.S. history, pits inner-city black residents against police; National Guard troops sent in by the Michigan governor and army soldiers deployed by the president; in five days of rioting, 43 people are killed, 467 injured, and more than 7,200 arrested, as well as some two thousand buildings destroyed.
1971	Henry Ford II announces a consortium of fifty area companies will build a $340 million center downtown on the banks of the Detroit River called the Renaissance Center.
1973–1974	The gasoline crises help give smaller, more fuel-efficient foreign-made cars a toehold in the United States, signaling a crisis for Detroit's automakers.
1976	The U.S. auto industry sinks further as more fuel-efficient cars from foreign manufacturers flood the market, creating layoffs as auto sales slump.
1976	Interagency Task Force for Detroit/Wayne County Riverfront Development completes study titled *The Land & the River* that inventoried riverfront lands and took stock of future possibilities beyond an industrial waterfront.
1977	The Renaissance Center's centerpiece is a seventy-three-story hotel, the tallest hotel in the world.
1979	Peter Stroh, a fourth-generation executive of the Stroh Brewing Company in Detroit, purchases the former World Headquarters of Parke, Davis & Company for mixed-use redevelopment as Stroh River Place.
1979–1980	City of Detroit develops a Linked Riverfront Parks Plan as a blueprint for creation of a system of riverfront parks linked by pedestrian trails; plan never materializes.
1982	Chene Park completed as a music and entertainment venue on the riverfront; constructed in support of Detroit's Linked Riverfront Parks Plan.
early-1980s	St. Aubin Marina constructed as one of the few public watercraft harbors along the Detroit River; constructed in support of Detroit's Linked Riverfront Parks Plan.
1983	Hudson's Department Store on Woodward Avenue closes.

1990	Southeast Michigan Greenways Initiative established to champion greenways.
1998	Detroit River designated an American Heritage River, with linked riverfront greenways becoming one of five priorities for the city.
1999	Stroh Brewing Company is sold to Pabst and Miller brewing companies.
1999	Publication of a report titled *Detroit's New Front Porch: A Riverfront Greenway in Southwest Detroit* that helped catalyze riverfront greenways.

SOURCES: "THE PEOPLE OF THE THREE FIRES (1600–1699)," DETROIT HISTORICAL MUSEUM, HTTP://DETROITHISTORICAL.ORG/LEARN/
TIMELINE-DETROIT; GAVRILOVICH AND MCGRAW 2000; HARTIG AND WALLACE 2015.

up perpendicular to the Detroit River. They typically extended two to three miles inland from the river. This gave river access to all landowners, increased variation in soil and drainage with a given lot, and increased efficiency in plowing by minimizing the number of times oxen teams had to be turned. These ribbon farms also fostered communication and socialization among farm families because houses were clustered at the ends of the lots. In 1748, settlers were offered inducements to come to Detroit, including a spade, an axe, a plough, a large wagon, a small wagon, seed, a cow, and a pig to be returned by the third harvest (Nolan 2000). By 1765 Detroit's population grew to eight hundred people, and Detroit became the largest city between Montreal and New Orleans.

Figure 9 shows how ribbon farms had established along much of Detroit's riverfront by 1796. Such agricultural practices were undoubtedly some of the first European impacts on the Detroit River shoreline and its coastal wetlands.

Detroit as a Way Station and Embarkation Point for Lands Further West

Cadillac understood clearly the importance of the Detroit River as a means of commerce, trade, and communication. As noted above, the first European impacts on the Detroit River shoreline were ribbon farms that began encroaching on its natural fringe of coastal wetlands. The British

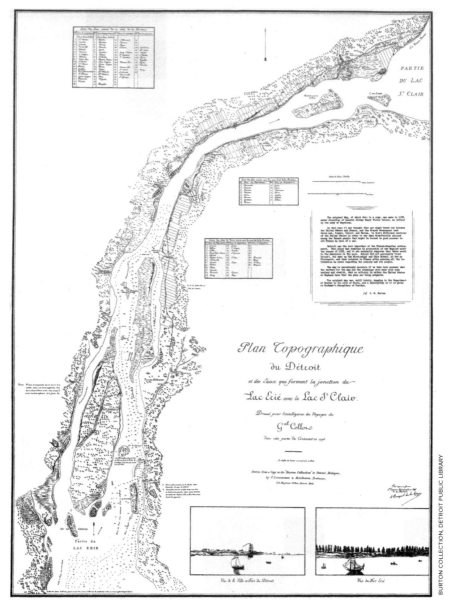

FIGURE 9. 1796 map of the Detroit River drafted by F. Leesmann and M.A. Heinze, Draftsmen, employed by the U.S. Engineer Office, Detroit.

established the first shipyard along the Detroit River (to produce naval vessels and commercial sailing craft) and constructed the first wharfs projecting into the Detroit River in 1760 and 1768, respectively (table 3). Additional wharfs were constructed in the 1780s and 1790s, including the Merchant's and King's Wharf in 1796.

Farmer (1890, 8), in his classic text *History of Detroit and Wayne County and Early Michigan*, noted:

> By the building of wharves and docks, and the extension of the shore by "made land," the river is continually encroached upon. At the foot of Woodward Avenue, it once came up seventy-seven feet north of the north line of Atwater Street; and beyond Woodward Avenue and Wayne Street it covered half the space occupied by the blocks between Atwater and Woodbridge Streets. At Cass Street it covered a part of what is now Jefferson Avenue.

On an early summer morning in 1805 the city of Detroit caught fire. This devastating fire began near the stables of John Harvey, the local baker. While no official cause was ever determined, it quickly spread to all the wooden structures of the city. At the time about six hundred people lived in Detroit. This fire destroyed all wooden structures in a single afternoon, but fortunately no one died. They went on to call it the Great Fire of 1805. After this fire, Gabriel Richard, the French Roman Catholic priest at St. Anne's Church, wrote Detroit's motto that still stands today: *Speramus meliora; resurget cineribus*, or "We hope for better days; it will arise from the ashes."

In reality, Detroit had been creeping toward the river for many years during the later eighteenth century. But soon after the Great Fire of 1805 the city was replatted, projecting lots into the Detroit River. These new platted lots, including a portion of the Detroit River, were now part of the city. Debris from the fire was used to help fill in the coastal wetlands of the Detroit River.

The physical configuration of Detroit's waterfront continued to change. In 1816, a wharf ten feet wide and extending two hundred feet into the Detroit River was authorized (Levanen 2000). Fees were fifty cents to tie a boat less than or equal to five tons, coming a distance of ten miles or more. Boats up to twenty-five tons were to pay $1.50, and larger draft had to pay $2.00.

In 1818, *Walk-in-the-Water*, the first steamboat on the upper Great Lakes, arrived in Detroit with much fanfare. Much of the city's population turned out for the historic arrival of this 150-passenger steamboat. Spectators lined the river, and she was welcomed with great ceremony (Hatcher 1945). One cannot emphasize enough the economic and social importance of this first visit by *Walk-in-the-Water*. It changed everyone's lives and opened opportunities. New settlers were encouraged to come to Detroit. The dreaded two-week voyage across Lake Erie was cut down to just a few days. Regular cruise schedules were now established between Buffalo, New York, and Detroit. Indeed, steamboat and sailing vessel traffic became so heavy that in 1819 the U.S. Congress declared the Detroit River a public highway (Levanen 2000).

Detroit's population increased from 900 in 1817 to 2,200 in 1830 to 9,700 in 1837. Waterborne commerce increased dramatically with the completion of the Erie Canal in 1825 (table 3). Prior to the completion of the Erie Canal, overland travel had been hard, hazardous, and quite expensive for commerce. Levanen (2000) reported that the cost of transporting a barrel of goods to Buffalo, New York, decreased from $5 in 1815 to $0.50 in 1825 because of the efficiencies of water transportation. Commerce grew consistently during the era. As Hatcher (1945, 181) notes, "Detroit, as both a way station and an embarkation point for lands farther west, felt the tremendous stirrings of the continent."

To supply facilities to meet this water transportation demand, Detroit continued its encroachment into the river. In 1827 the Detroit City Council voted to improve its waterfront facilities with a sixty-foot-wide dock at the foot of Woodward Avenue. By September 1827, the *Detroit*

FIGURE 10. Map of Detroit showing the Detroit River shoreline prior to the Great Fire of 1805 and the line of the wharf in 1889.

Gazette reported the successful completion of this embankment project (as it was called at that time) that now provided a convenient safe landing for vessels and that improved the "filthiness" associated with the wharves that was perceived to be causing waterborne diseases (Dunnigan 2001). During this project and at the same time that they were demolishing Fort Shelby, abandoned earth works from the fort were also used to fill in the riverfront, in addition to debris from the Great Fire of 1805.

The extent of this embankment project is captured in figure 10 that clearly shows the Detroit River shoreline prior to the Great Fire of 1805 (located a fair distance inland) and the new shoreline of 1889 (at the very bottom of the figure) demonstrating human encroachment of an estimated 0.3 mile into the river. A combination of timber framing and earth was used to create new waterfront facilities (i.e., wharf) at the expense of the river's wetland and riparian habitats.

It would not be until the 1890s that the U.S. Army Corps of Engineers would initially establish harbor lines in the Detroit River to regulate where piers and other structures could be built. During this time shoreline filling activities were allowed landward of harbor lines without federal approval or authorization. This policy became official in 1899 with the signing of the Rivers and Harbors Act. Section 10 of this act prohibited the creation of any obstruction not authorized by Congress to the navigable capacity of any waters of the United States. Further, it stated that is was unlawful to "build or commence the building of any wharf, pier, dolphin, boom, weir, breakwater, bulkhead, jetty, or other structures in any port, roadstead, haven, harbor, canal, navigable river, or other water of the United States, outside established harbor lines." Levanen (2000) reported that during the late 1800s five miles of Detroit River waterfront were lined with docks.

To help better understand why the natural shoreline of the Detroit River was substantially altered it is worth providing some insights into Detroit as a center of commerce. It was between 1850 and 1870 that Detroit reached a high plateau of commercial development where

TABLE 4. Principal Industries of Detroit in 1860

INDUSTRY	VALUE OF PRODUCTS ($)
Copper Smelting	1,500,000
Lumber Sawed	619,049
Machinery (steam engines, etc.)	608,478
Iron (bar and railroad)	585,000
Leather	380,225
Flour and Meal	313,837
Liquors, Malt	262,163
Pig Iron	145,000
Furs	143,000
Soaps and Candles	137,915
Printing	136,400
Boots and Shoes	131,852
Sashes, Doors, and Blinds	126,929
Bread and Crackers	99,200

SOURCE: HOLLI 1976.

out-of-state business with agricultural settlements had replaced fur trade as the primary business. Table 4 depicts this shift in commerce with the list of principal industries in Detroit in 1860. Detroit was now primarily a commercial city. Holli (1976) noted that well before Detroit became an industrial superpower and the Motor City, it was a leading city of commerce. Detroit's primary processing industries and trade serving manufactures during 1850–70 provided the knowledge and were the building blocks for a factory town that mass-produced automobiles (Holli 1976).

Detroit during 1850–70 was now a mercantile city with wholesale trading and retailing as its two top functions. An informative description of a typical Detroit business establishment during this time was provided by Roberts (1855, 18):

The store has a free stone front, is four stories high, occupies a front of fifty feet and extending in depth one hundred feet, comprising ten rooms, each twenty-five feet in width and one hundred feet in depth and an area of 25,000 square feet, all of which are filled to their utmost capacity with foreign and domestic dry goods, carpets, cloths, millinery and clothing—in addition to which the firm occupies a store-house in the rear. The retail rooms are four in number, furnished in the most gorgeous style. About three hundred gas lights are required to light the several apartments. From sixty to seventy-five salesmen and from one hundred to one hundred and fifty persons altogether are employed in the several departments, and including those outside seamsters and seamstresses, the firm gives employment to about six hundred persons. Their invoices of merchandise imported during the year 1854 amounted to more than seven hundred thousand dollars. This store was recently refitted and opened for the fall trade with an invoice of goods amounting to over four hundred thousand dollars.

Shipping during this era increased in direct proportion to the increase in commerce. In 1850 a total of 2,341 vessels carrying a total of 671,545 tons passed through the port of Detroit. By 1907, this total increased to 75,000,000 tons. Detroit remained a vibrant port of call and a marketplace for domestic goods throughout the 1800s. However, with the construction of the St. Lawrence Seaway, beginning in 1855 with construction of the first lock in Sault Ste. Marie, Detroit soon became a center for trade and one of the busiest ports in the world.

It should also be noted that three creeks—Savoyard Creek, May's Creek, and Bloody Run—ran through old Detroit and emptied into the Detroit River (Hudgins 1946). Savoyard Creek, in its early days, was a meandering 1.25-mile creek with reeds and rushes, and a willow swamp as its headwaters (Farmer 1890). With the growth of Detroit, it became an open sewer and so offensive and malodorous that the city converted it into a covered sewer in 1836 (Farmer 1890). May's Creek was approximately 2.5 miles in length and provided enough water to run a grist mill six to eight months per year (Hudgins 1946). Bloody Run was a 3.5-mile creek named after the defeat of Captain Dalyell and the slaughter of a large part of his company by Indians in 1863. Each of these creeks was either filled in or covered over to make way for streets and building sites in Detroit. Hudgins (1946, 348) notes that these three streams "buoyed up canoes, turned mill wheels, drained the land, formed barriers against encroachment of enemies, required bridging, became polluted nuisances, and at last were filled and graded with much labor and expense." Not only were these streams lost to development, but their floodplains and wetlands were destroyed, eliminating the ecosystem services or life-sustaining benefits they provided to Detroit.

Manufacturing

Detroit's population grew from approximately 45,000 in 1860 to over 285,000 in 1900 (Dunbar 1965). Much of this growth was attributed to the development and growth of manufacturing. Dunbar (1965, 584) provides important insights on the growth of Detroit into a manufacturing giant and why this happened:

> The easy availability of iron, copper, lead, wood, and other raw materials had much to do with the location of important manufactures. Boxes and barrels for shipping were cheap at Detroit; coal had to be shipped a relatively short distance; railroad and water transport facilities were excellent. By 1880 it was estimated that almost $16 million was invested in manufacturing plants, and that the annual product was worth $35 million. Iron and steel industries were the most important Detroit industries in the 1880s. The largest factory for the manufacture of railroad cars and car wheels in the nation was located at Detroit. Immense stove factories, notably the Detroit Stove Company, the Peninsular Stove Company, and

the Michigan Stove Company, were front-rank industries. Parke, Davis, and Company, famed maker of pharmaceuticals, had its beginning in Detroit in 1867. In 1880 over sixty establishments manufactured chewing tobacco and cigars, and the city was one of the largest manufacturers of chewing tobacco in the country. The shoe factory in which Hazen S. Pingree made his fortune was the largest of its kind west of New York. D.M. Ferry and Company was the leading concern in the growing and distribution of seeds. The 919 manufacturing establishments in Detroit in 1880 employed some 16,000 persons.

In direct response to Detroit's strategic location in the heart of the Great Lakes, the demand for transportation of passengers and goods, and the availability of essential resources, Detroit also became one of the greatest shipbuilding ports in the United States (Hartig 2003).

The Detroit Dry Dock was incorporated in 1872 by Captain Stephen Kirby and was located at Atwater and Orleans Streets. In 1877, the company grew by buying Wyandotte Shipbuilding, which was supervised by Captain Kirby's son, Frank. From then on until 1929, the Detroit Dry Dock Company ran the two shipyards that built hundreds of vessels, from lake steamers to railroad ferries.

The Dry Dock Engine Works was very well known for manufacturing and repairing marine steam engines and boilers for Great Lakes freighters and passenger vessels. It began producing marine steam engines as early as 1867 (Klug 2002). The steam engine was the hallmark of the industrial age. Application of steam-engine technology to ships and boats transformed communications, transportation, and warfare throughout the world. In the Great Lakes basin, steam engines revolutionized the business of transporting passengers and raw materials, notably iron ore. The transformation of the United States into an industrial power at the end of the nineteenth century in no small measure rested on the conversion of iron ore into castings and useful iron or steel shapes (Klug 2002). It is important to note that Henry Ford worked for the Dry Dock

Engine Works from 1880 to 1882 as an apprentice machinist. Ford's work with steam engines at this company helped inspire his idea for adding an engine to a carriage for road use.

In 1899, Detroit Dry Dock was sold to the American Shipbuilding Company, consolidating the Orleans Street facilities and the Wyandotte yards and renaming it the Detroit Shipbuilding Company. These operations succumbed to the recession of the 1920s, with the Wyandotte yard closing in 1922 and the Orleans Street yard closing in 1929.

Henry Ford built his first car in 1896, followed by Ransom E. Olds opening Detroit's first automobile manufacturing plant in 1899 (table 3). Henry Ford then introduced the assembly line in 1913. In 1904, 3.8 percent of Detroit's 60,554 industrial employees were employed in the automobile industry (Holli 1976). By 1919, 45 percent of Detroit's 308,520 industrial employees were employed in the automobile industry (Holli 1976). Detroit was now the Motor City and one of the largest industrial manufacturing centers in the world.

By the middle of the twentieth century one in six American jobs were connected to the automobile industry, and the Motor City was its epicenter (Martelle 2012). It should be no surprise that Detroit reached the apex of its population growth in 1950 with 1.85 million people. Through this time the shoreline of the Detroit River was consistently improved/altered to meet the needs of industry and commerce. By 1982, most of the Detroit River shoreline on the U.S. mainland had been hardened with concrete and steel, providing no habitat value (Manny 2003). Further, 97 percent of the historical coastal wetlands that existed along the Michigan mainland of the Detroit River in 1815 were converted into other land uses (Manny 2003).

Industrial Decline and Becoming a Poster Child for the Rust Belt

Since the 1950s, Detroit experienced considerable loss of population (over a 60 percent decline since 1950) and industry, rising unemployment, increased cost of living, decreased access to city services, and increased crime. To many, it became the stereotypical image of the Rust Belt. This decline of industry loss of people and jobs, and associated other socioeconomic problems culminated in Detroit's bankruptcy in 2013.

By the 1970s and 1980s, a considerable portion of Detroit's waterfront land between the MacArthur Bridge to the 980-acre island park called Belle Isle and the Ambassador Bridge to Canada was either abandoned buildings, underutilized street parking lots, material storage piles, or cement silos that prohibited access to the Detroit River (Hartig and Wallace 2015). Public access was very limited (figure 11). For over a century, city planners identified the highest and best use of this land to be "industrial" because of obvious revenue returns (Hartig and Wallace 2015). Detroit was an industrial town, and it had a working riverfront that supported industry and commerce. However, times had changed. There were now fewer people and industries and much underutilized and undervalued riverfront land. Detroit citizens had literally lost their connection to the Detroit River.

Concluding Remarks

European settlement and the growth of Detroit into the fourth largest city in the United States in 1950 with 1.85 million people that provided 296,000 manufacturing jobs caused substantial changes in Detroit's riverfront and contributed substantially to the loss of most of its coastal wetlands located along Michigan's mainland. But along with Detroit's industrial and urban expansion also came substantial water pollution

DETROIT RIVERFRONT CONSERVANCY

FIGURE 11. Detroit riverfront in the late 1990s showing limited public access and much underutilized land.

that eventually received considerable public outrage and media attention. This pollution had to be addressed to realize the full potential of Detroit's riverfront. Public outcry against this water pollution was growing, beginning in the 1960s. Could Detroit rise to the challenge, with the help of citizen outcry, federal and state laws, and international treaties?

CHAPTER 3

Detroit River Revival

t was 1960 and twelve years after eleven thousand waterfowl died in the Detroit River from oil pollution, an event credited with starting the industrial pollution control program of Michigan. The Detroit River was still in a deplorable and grossly polluted state and considered one of the most polluted rivers in the United States. Just when everyone hoped it would never happen again, another winter waterfowl die-off due to oil pollution occurred in 1960 killing twelve thousand birds (Hartig and Stafford 2003). Following the 1960 winter waterfowl die-off due to oil pollution, another one happened in 1967 killing 5,400 birds.

For many, the 1960s was a decade of a public awakening of how humans were polluting the very ecosystems that they lived in. During the 1960s, increasing inputs of phosphorus to Lake Erie led to excessive algal growth, oxygen depletion in the deeper waters of the lake, and massive fish kills. Picture front-end loaders, the kind you see being used on highway construction projects, removing decomposing aquatic plants, algae, and dead fish from bathing beaches on Lake Erie.

Such widespread pollution of Lake Erie and its tributaries was prominently featured in national magazines, including *Time* magazine on August 20, 1965. In an article titled "Ecology: Time for Transfusion," *Time* reported:

> Lake Erie is critically ill, and the symptoms are there for all to see. Beaches that once were gleaming with white sand are covered with smelly greenish slime. The lake's prize fish—walleyes, blue pike, yellow perch and whitefish—have all but disappeared, and the fishing fleets along with them.

The national media coverage of the deterioration of Lake Erie, especially the dead fish and decomposing plants that were off-gassing hydrogen sulfide (i.e., the smell of rotten eggs) led journalists to conclude that "Lake Erie is dead" (Leach 1999, 11). Public outcry over the widespread pollution of Lake Erie was growing.

It was also during this time that Rachel Carson published a book titled *Silent Spring* (1962) that chronicled the hazards of pesticides like DDT, including how these toxic substances were biomagnifying up food webs and jeopardizing the health of countless species, from tiny warblers to birds of prey to humans. This book questioned humanity's faith in technological progress and became a powerful influence in the creation of the environmental movement.

Then in 1969 both the Rouge River (a tributary of the Detroit River) in Detroit and the Cuyahoga River in Cleveland, Ohio, caught on fire and ignited a national outrage over water pollution. The Cuyahoga River fire, in particular, came precisely at the right time when national media began to cover the neglect of the environment in a big way and helped awaken the nation to widespread environmental degradation (Hartig 2010). The Cuyahoga River fire went on to become the poster child of the environmental movement. Numerous citizens and stakeholder groups were outraged at the gross pollution and deplorable state of Lake Erie

FIGURE 12. McClouth Steel Corporation discharging oil into the Detroit River in Trenton, Michigan, 1960.

FIGURE 13. Water pollution of the Detroit River coming from the submerged outfall of the Detroit Wastewater Treatment Plant and from the Rouge River, 1966.

and its tributaries like the Detroit and Cuyahoga rivers (figures 12 and 13) and voiced their opposition at public water pollution hearings convened across the country, including ones in Detroit, Michigan, and Buffalo, New York. But soon there would be another environmental crisis that would shake the community foundation and further elevate the public outcry over pollution.

In 1967 a young Norwegian graduate student named Norvald Fimreite came to the University of Western Ontario to study contaminant impacts on wildlife. Fimreite had studied mercury contamination found in Japan and Sweden during the 1950s and early 1960s and was investigating whether or not a similar situation was occurring in the Great Lakes. He estimated that in the late 1960s approximately one-half pound of mercury was lost to the St. Clair River (a connecting channel linking Lake Huron to Lake St. Clair that empties into the Detroit River) for every one ton of chlorine produced at Dow Chemical of Canada's chlor-alkali plant in Sarnia, Ontario (Turney 1971). Government scientists went on to discover that, in total, over 200,600 pounds of mercury were discharged into the St. Clair River, with additional amounts of mercury discharged into the Detroit River from Wyandotte Chemical Company. Fimreite followed up by sampling fish from Lake St. Clair in 1970 and found mercury concentrations over four times the standard for safe human consumption.

This news of mercury contamination of the St. Clair River and downstream environments, including the Detroit River, descended on the people of Michigan and Ontario "like a thunder clap" (Turney 1971, 1427). Mercury had contaminated the St. Clair River, Lake St. Clair, Detroit River, and western Lake Erie. The entire fishery from the St. Clair River to Lake Erie had to be closed, including shutting down forty small family fisheries harvesting $1–2 million worth of fish each year (Hartig 1983). This news of this mercury contamination catapulted across North America like a projectile shot from a slingshot. It went on to be called the "Mercury Crisis of 1970."

This public outcry over the pollution of the Detroit River and Lake Erie, the publishing of *Silent Spring* (Carson 1962), the burning of the Rouge and Cuyahoga rivers, and the "Mercury Crisis of 1970" collectively went on to be the catalyst for the establishment of Earth Day in 1970, the Canada Water Act in 1970, the U.S. Clean Water Act in 1972, the U.S.–Canada Great Lakes Water Quality Agreement of 1972, and the 1973 U.S. Endangered Species Act.

The enactment of these laws and the work under the Great Lakes Water Quality Agreement stimulated many pollution prevention and control programs. This also initiated a long history of Canada–U.S. cooperation in investigating and monitoring the Detroit River–western Lake Erie corridor. Indeed, the various laws and agreements established to curb water pollution have over a forty-five-year history.

The Detroit River was clearly under the microscope with many governmental monitoring programs, but also many university, industrial, and nongovernmental monitoring initiatives. Collectively, these monitoring programs have documented substantial environmental improvements since the 1960s:

- over a 97 percent reduction in oil releases
- over a 96 percent decrease in phosphorus discharges
- a 4,600 tons/day decrease in chloride discharges
- a substantial improvement in municipal wastewater treatment by upgrading all plants from primary treatment to secondary treatment with phosphorus removal
- a 95 percent reduction in untreated waste from combined sewer overflow discharges (i.e., in sewerage systems that carry both sanitary sewage and stormwater runoff, the portion of the flow that goes untreated to receiving rivers or lakes because of wastewater treatment plant overloading during storms)
- an 85 percent reduction in mercury in fish
- a 91 percent decline in PCBs (i.e., Arochlor 1260), a 92

percent decline in DDE, and a 94 percent decline in 2,3,7,8-tetrachlorordibenzo-p-dioxin in herring gull eggs from Fighting Island (de Solla et al. 2015)

- the remediation of one million cubic yards of contaminated sediment at a cost of over $154 million (Hartig et al. 2009).

The combined effect of these environmental improvements over the last forty-five years has been a surprising ecological recovery.

Recovery of Bald Eagles

Bald eagles (*Haliaeetus leucocephalus*) are one of the most recognizable birds in the United States. They have been the national emblem of the United States since 1782 and a spiritual symbol for Native Americans for even longer. As adults, these regal birds have white-feathered heads that gleam against their chocolate-brown bodies and wings. They have an eight-foot wingspan, piercing eyes, a massive hooked beak, and powerful talons to aid in hunting for prey like small mammals, birds, and fish.

During the early 1900s, bald eagles were "evenly distributed" throughout Michigan (Best and Wilke 2007). The population then declined through the mid-1900s due to loss of nesting habitat and persecution by humans (i.e., shooting, poisoning, trapping, and electrocution). In the 1950s this decline of eagles in Michigan accelerated until they were near extinction in the 1970s. This trend was similar throughout the lower forty-eight states and southern Canada. This bald eagle decline was a result of several factors, most influential being the biomagnification of organochlorine compounds such as DDT and PCBs following World War II (Colborn 1991, Bowerman et al. 1995, Bowerman et al. 1998, Bowerman et al. 2002). Avian exposure to these contaminants has caused reproductive failure, sterility, life-threatening deformities such as crossed bills and eggshell thinning, altered behavior such as impaired foraging

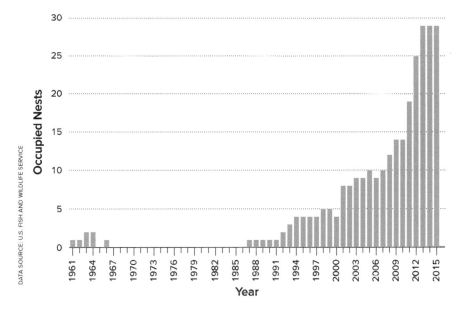

FIGURE 14. Number of occupied bald eagle nests in southeast Michigan, 1961–2015.

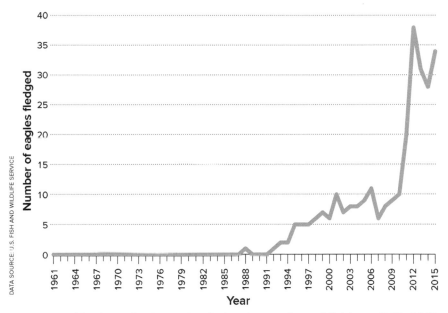

FIGURE 15. Number of bald eagles fledged in southeast Michigan, 1961–2015.

abilities, and increased susceptibility to disease through immune system dysfunction, and has even resulted in death in cases of acute poisoning (Best and Wilke 2007).

From 1961 to 1987 there were no bald eagles produced in metropolitan Detroit due primarily to organochlorine contamination (figures 14 and 15). Since 1991, there has been a steady increase in the number of occupied bald eagle nests per year in metropolitan Detroit to where today twenty-five or more active nests have been documented during 2012–15. This nesting success has resulted in the fledgling of twenty-eight or more young per year during 2012–15.

Recovery of Peregrine Falcons

Peregrine falcons (*Falco columbarius*) are regarded by falconers and biologists alike as one of the noblest and most spectacular of all birds of prey. They have never been very abundant anywhere in the world due to very specific nest site requirements and their position at the top of the food web. Their habitat includes cliffs of mountains and coastlines, open country, and sometimes even cities. As peregrine falcons became limited by availability of nest sites and prey, they often moved into cities, nesting on building ledges and feeding on pigeons.

Peregrine falcons are one of the fastest birds in the world, possibly reaching two hundred miles per hour. During the 1940s-1970s, the world population of peregrines was decimated, mostly due to the use of pesticides like DDT (Tordoff and Redig 1997). When DDE, the breakdown product of DDT, accumulates in the bodies of many birds, it causes them to lay very thin-shelled eggs that break during incubation (Becher and Hartig 2017). Studies show the peregrine falcon retains the highest DDT residue of all vertebrates, causing reproductive problems (Appel et al. 2002). A repeat of the 1940 survey of historically known aeries (i.e., nest sites), conducted in 1964, found no breeding pairs or even single adult peregrines east of the Mississippi River. As a result, the peregrine falcon was listed as an endangered species by the U.S. Fish and Wildlife Service in 1970.

By the 1970s, DDT had been banned in both Europe and the U.S., partially due to data linking it to the decline of the peregrine falcon. In 1981, the Midwest Peregrine Falcon Restoration Team was created and charged with the task of developing a management plan to restore peregrine falcons as a nesting bird population in the upper Midwest.

Peregrine falcon reintroductions in the Midwest began in 1982. Peregrine chicks of captive adults were raised in artificial structures and subsequently released into their new urban environment. These new homes, including buildings of all shapes and sizes, bridges, and power plant stacks, all have success stories, so that in 2005, over ninety cities had peregrine falcon nesting efforts recorded in the Midwest. Peregrines feed exclusively on other birds that are abundant in urban areas, such as pigeons, mourning doves, starlings, flickers, and woodcocks (Appel et al. 2002). It is also thought that as these urban-raised peregrines expanded their territories, they would naturally seek out some of the natural, more traditional sites, such as cliffs in the Upper Peninsula of Michigan.

In 1987, five peregrine falcon young were released in downtown Detroit by the Michigan Department of Natural Resources. In 1988, one subadult pair was present when the five chicks were released; however, this pair did not successfully nest. For the next four years various pairs continued to visit each year with no nesting success. Then, in 1993, two young peregrines were successfully raised for the first time documented in Detroit's history, and the first in the Lower Peninsula in thirty-seven years. The number of nesting sites in southeast Michigan, including the Ambassador Bridge, has increased from one in 1989 92 to thirteen to twenty in 2011–15. Further, the number of young produced in southeast Michigan increased from none in 1992 to twenty-one to thirty per year in 2011–15 (figure 16). The goal of the Michigan Department of Natural

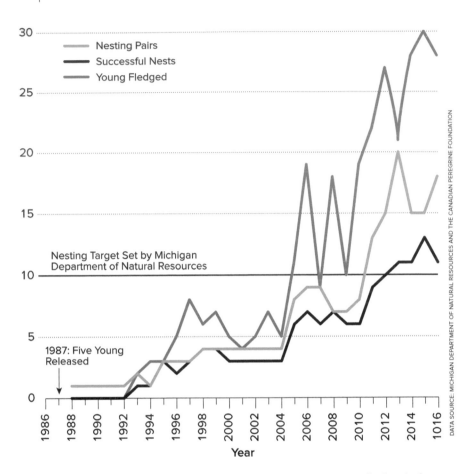

FIGURE 16. Trends in nesting pairs, successful nests, and young fledged of peregrine falcons in southeast Michigan, 1987–2015.

Resources' Natural Heritage Program (nongame wildlife)—to maintain a population of at least ten nesting pairs of peregrine falcons in Michigan—has now been met.

The year 1999 will always be remembered as a milestone year for the restoration of peregrine falcons. On August 20, it soared off the list of federally endangered species. Today, it is a true conservation success story.

Recovery of Osprey

Osprey (*Pandion haliaetus*) are found worldwide and are a common sight soaring over shorelines, patrolling waterways, and standing on their large stick nests with their white heads gleaming. Also known as "fish hawks," "river hawks," and "sea hawks," they are one of the largest birds of prey in North America with a nearly six-foot wingspan. They feed almost exclusively on fish and are considered a good indicator of aquatic ecosystem health.

Osprey is a superb predator on fish. They fly or hover some thirty to one hundred feet above the water surface, then plunge feetfirst into the water in search of their prey. They use gripping pads on their feet and curved claws to help pluck fish from the water and carry them off for great distances.

Osprey has been designated as a "species of special concern" in Michigan. As with bald eagles and peregrine falcons, a dramatic decline of osprey occurred throughout North America due to widespread use of DDT and other organochlorine pesticides that caused eggshell thinning.

In the early 1960s, the osprey population in Michigan was rapidly declining (Postupalsky 1977). By 1999 there was only one active nest in southern Michigan. To restore the osprey population, the Michigan Department of Natural Resources, with assistance from the Huron Clinton Metropolitan Authority, the Detroit Zoological Society, and DTE Energy, established the Osprey Reintroduction Project of Southern Michigan (Michigan Department of Natural Resources 1998). The goal of this Osprey Reintroduction Program was thirty nesting pairs in the southern half of Michigan's Lower Peninsula by 2020. This project involved moving fifty chicks from the northern parts of the state to areas in southern Michigan.

There are now more than thirty known nests in the southern Lower Peninsula, plus dozens of nests in the northern Lower Peninsula and the Upper Peninsula. Michigan Osprey, a citizen organization devoted

FIGURE 17. An osprey feeding young at the Strong Unit of the Detroit River International Wildlife Refuge.

to tracking and restoring the osprey population, has reported that the goal of thirty nesting pairs in the southern half of the Lower Peninsula was achieved in 2010, ten years ahead of schedule. In southeast Michigan alone (i.e., Wayne, Macomb, Oakland, Livingston, Washtenaw, Monroe, and St. Clair counties), there were thirty-eight, fifty, and fifty-two nesting pairs in 2015, 2016, and 2017, respectively (figure 17). It is interesting to note that in 2009 a pair of osprey built a nest in a cell phone tower adjacent to the Gibraltar Wetlands Unit of the Detroit River International Wildlife Refuge along the lower Detroit River, representing the first time that osprey have successfully nested in Wayne County since the 1890s.

Clearly, this osprey reintroduction program has been successful, but concerns remain. Osprey still need to be protected from killing or capture, especially in their wintering grounds in Florida, the southwestern United States, and Central America. For example, an osprey named Monroe Spark that fledged from the Detroit River International Wildlife Refuge's Strong Unit in 2013 was fitted with a backpack satellite transmitter that tracked it to Cuba where it was probably killed by a fish farmer. This shows that international efforts are needed to protect this species. Some protection is provided to osprey under the Migratory Bird Treaty Act of 1918; however, greater international cooperation is needed. With help and support from everyone, the osprey will continue to be an awe-inspiring sight.

Return of Lake Whitefish

Lake whitefish (*Coregonus clupeaformis*) is a prized commercial species and a key indicator of ecosystem health. During the late nineteenth and early twentieth centuries, large numbers of lake whitefish entered the Detroit River in the fall to spawn. Whitefish are known to spawn on rock, honeycomb limestone, gravel, and sand substrates.

Historical commercial fishing harvest records showed that lake whitefish harvest in the Detroit River exceeded a half million pounds in the late 1800s and collapsed during the early part of the twentieth century. Loss of spawning and nursery habitat and overfishing were identified as key factors in the decline of the population.

The most dramatic example of lake whitefish spawning habitat destruction was the construction of the shipping channels in the Detroit River. Millions of tons of limestone bedrock, cobble, and gravel were removed from the lower Detroit River to create the shipping channels to support commerce. These rock and gravel substrates provided critical spawning habitats for lithophilic (i.e., rock loving) broadcast spawning fishes like lake whitefish, lake sturgeon (*Acipenser fulvescens*), walleye (*Sander vitreus*), and others. The creation of shipping channels began in 1874 with the construction of the Limekiln Crossing and continued on through the early 1900s with the construction of the Livingstone and Amherstburg Channels (Bennion and Manny 2011). The construction of the Livingstone Channel was particularly damaging to spawning habitat.

An 11.8-mile channel (minimum width 300 feet; minimum depth 22 feet) was created in a limestone bedrock sill at the mouth of the Detroit River to facilitate shipping. This construction of the Livingstone Channel not only destroyed whitefish spawning habitat, but altered river hydrology creating a disconnect between the spawning areas in the Detroit River and the nursery areas in western Lake Erie.

Spawning runs of lake whitefish into the Detroit River nearly disappeared by the early 1900s (Trautman 1957, Goodyear et al. 1982, Hartman 1972). By the 1960s and 1970s lake whitefish were at an all-time low for a variety of reasons: overexploitation, predation by and competition with invasive species, degradation of water quality and habitat, and the loss of an important member of the zooplankton called *Diporeia,* a major nutrient-rich food source of lake whitefish (due to the introduction of zebra and/or quagga mussels).

The lake whitefish population of Lake Erie began to recover in the early 1980s. Then in 2006, whitefish spawning in the Detroit River was documented for the first time since 1916, aiding in the recovery of the population (Roseman et al. 2012). Recent research has quantified the annual export of lake whitefish larvae and that the majority of lake whitefish larvae are exported through the highest volume channels of the Detroit River, including Trenton, Livingstone, and Amherstburg. Total annual export of lake whitefish larvae ranged from 28.8 million in 2010 to 83.4 million in 2011, primarily through the Trenton and Amherstburg channels (about 70 percent) (Roseman et al. 2017).

Return of Lake Sturgeon

During the 1800s, lake sturgeon was one of the most abundant fish species in the Detroit River. The relationship between lake sturgeon and humans during the 1800s was accurately described as "kaleidoscopic" (Scott and Crossman 1973). Before the 1860s commercial fishermen slaughtered lake sturgeon as a nuisance fish because they became entangled in nets and because they sucked up spawn (Bogue 2000). During this era, lake sturgeon were even stacked like firewood and left to dry on the banks of the Detroit River in Amherstburg, Ontario, to be later burned in the boilers of steamboats (Bein 2012).

It was during the mid-1860s that the economic value of lake sturgeon was recognized when their eggs became sought after as caviar and their smoked flesh was craved as a delicacy. This led to the development of an important commercial fishery. Total lake sturgeon harvest peaked in the mid-1880s at 8.6 million pounds.

During the late 1800s, the corridor between Lakes Huron and Erie was one of the most productive waters for lake sturgeon in North America. It should be no surprise that during this era the Detroit River was recognized as one of the best lake sturgeon fisheries in the United States. According to the *Detroit Free Press* (1903), Detroiters had the satisfaction of knowing that they got the best sturgeon steaks and the best caviar in the world caught in the neighborhood of the city.

Populations continued to decline and were nearly extirpated by the middle of the twentieth century (Roseman et al. 2011). In more recent years, the lake sturgeon population in Michigan was estimated to be about 1 percent of its former abundance (Tody 1974).

From the 1970s to 1999 no lake sturgeon spawning was reported in the Detroit River. Again, it was just a century earlier that it was one of the most productive sturgeon spawning grounds in the United States. To scientists' surprise, in 2001 lake sturgeon spawning was documented on a coal cinder pile near Zug Island in the Detroit River for the first time in over twenty years (Caswell et al. 2004). These scientists believed that sturgeon productivity was now most limited by habitat. In response, lake sturgeon spawning habitat was created in nine locations in the river: McKee Park in Windsor, Ontario, in 2003; Belle Isle in Detroit, Michigan, in 2004 and 2016; Fort Malden in Amherstburg, Ontario, in 2004; BASF property along the Trenton Channel in Riverview, Michigan, in 2008;

Fighting Island in 2008 and expanded in 2013; Grassy Island in 2015; and off Historic Fort Wayne in 2018. The Fighting Island, Grassy Island, and 2016 Belle Isle reefs were successful, with lake sturgeon spawning the first spring after construction. Recent fishery assessments have estimated the lake sturgeon population in the Detroit River at 6,360 (95 percent confidence interval: 3,106–13,599 fish) (Chiotti et al. 2012). Clearly, the future of this threatened species is very promising.

Return of Walleye

Walleye is the largest member of the perch family, and few fish match the walleye for the combination of recreational angling enjoyment and table fare. Indeed, the Detroit River and Lake Erie are considered the "Walleye Capital of the World." It is estimated that ten million walleye ascend the Detroit River from Lake Erie each spring to spawn, creating an internationally renowned sport fishery. As adults, walleye are terminal predators in the Detroit River food web and a key indicator of ecological health.

Since 1978 the Lake Erie Committee of the Great Lakes Fishery Commission has been estimating walleye population size in Lake Erie using systematic monitoring and mathematical modeling. In 1978, the Lake Erie walleye population was estimated at less than ten million (ages two years old and greater) and considered in a "crisis" state (Lake Erie Walleye Task Group 2005). The population has generally increased over time, but with some year-to-year variability. In 2016, the Lake Erie Committee of the Great Lakes Fishery Commission estimated the size of the west-central population at 30.626 million age two and older walleye (Lake Erie Walleye Task Group 2017). This represents a healthy fishery according to the Lake Erie Committee that has recommended that the walleye population should be maintained between twenty-five and forty million fish ("maintenance level").

Return of Beaver

Beaver (*Castor canadensis*) is the largest rodent in North America and the official symbol of Canada. Beaver were extirpated from the region during the fur trade era. It should also be noted that during the height of oil pollution in the 1940s–1970s, beaver could not have survived in the Detroit River because oil would have matted their fur and they would have lost their ability to trap air and water to maintain body temperature. Loss of riparian forest habitat was another contributing factor. Then in 2008, two inquisitive beaver probably swam over from the Canadian side of Lake St. Clair, built a lodge at DTE Energy's Conner Creek Power Plant, and produced two pups in 2009. This represented the first time that beaver were reported in the Detroit River since 1877 (Johnson 1919), representing a 131-year absence.

Beavers have also been reported from at least six other locations in the Detroit River watershed, including Belle Isle, the headwaters of the Rouge River, in the Rouge River near the University of Michigan–Dearborn, at Crosswinds Marsh, at DTE's Rouge Power Plant in River Rouge, and Grosse Ile. Although the return of a few beavers cannot be considered ecologically significant, it is of great public interest and provides supporting anecdotal evidence of improvement.

Return of Mayflies

Mayflies (*Hexagenia* spp.) are a type of insect that spends its juvenile life in the water and its adult life in the air and on land. They have long been used by resource managers as an indicator of aquatic ecosystem health. In western Lake Eire, mayfly populations were extirpated in the 1940s and 1950s as a result of water pollution. Mayflies then reappeared in sediments of western Lake Erie in 1992–93 after a forty-year absence (Schloesser and Krieger 2007). They returned in response to improved water quality resulting from pollution prevention and control programs, along with changes in trophic status, ascribed to invasive zebra and quagga mussels.

Some of the earliest Great Lakes macrobenthic invertebrate surveys were conducted in 1929–30 by Wright and Tidd (1933), including the mouth of the Detroit River. During these surveys, mayfly larvae were conspicuously absent from the mouth of the Detroit River, indicating light to moderate pollution at the river mouth.

Pollution control programs put in place starting in the 1970s have resulted in improved water and sediment quality in many areas of the Detroit River. In general, mayfly larvae abundance has increased in the Detroit River in recent years, particularly in areas not substantially impacted by pollution (e.g., the head of the Detroit River and portions of the Canadian side of the river) (Ciborowski 2007). However, areas of the river still impacted by pollution continue to show low mayfly larvae abundance, particularly downstream of the confluence of the Rouge River and the Trenton Channel.

It is interesting to note that improvements in Detroit River water quality have also been reflected in the numbers of night-flying mayflies that are attracted to streetlights and storefronts along the river during warm summer evenings. Kovats, Ciborowski, and Corkum (1996) have documented an increase in flying adult stages of *Hexagenia* along both the Canadian and U.S. sides of the river in recent years.

Challenges and the Need for Sustained Monitoring and Research

This ecological recovery is remarkable, but monitoring and surveillance programs in this corridor have also documented a number of environmental and natural resource challenges. Six of the most pressing ones include human population growth, transportation expansion, and land use changes; nonpoint source pollution; toxic substances contamination;

habitat loss and degradation; introduction of exotic species; and green-house gases and global warming (Hartig et al. 2009).

Clearly, more needs to be done to fully realize long-term goals of restoring the physical, chemical, and biological integrity of the Detroit River. However, the progress achieved to date, the informed, engaged, and vocal stakeholders and nongovernmental organizations involved, and the broad-based desire to create a sense of place in these watersheds bodes well for further improvement and recovery. Scientists continue to worry about societal complacency (Hartig 2014). The 1960s were clearly an environmental tipping point when there was an urgent need to prevent and control pollution. If appropriate action was not taken, society could see irreversible damage or harm to our ecosystems. We cannot afford to reach another tipping point. We need to make sure that we sustain our research and monitoring programs, ensure that they are closely coupled with management efforts (in the spirit of adaptive management that assesses status, sets priorities, and takes action in an iterative fashion for continuous improvement), and that the resulting scientific information and knowledge are translated for decision-makers and laypersons and are broadly disseminated. We need to continue to remediate and restore these ecosystems using all tools in our collective toolbox, including actions by households and individuals. We also need to invest in capacity building, sustain and indeed grow our nongovern-mental organizations, and place a higher priority on education to help develop the next generation of environmentalists, conservationists, and sustainability entrepreneurs.

Concluding Remarks

In the late 1960s when the Detroit River was considered one of the most polluted rivers in North America, no bald eagles, peregrine falcons, or osprey were reproducing in the Detroit River watershed, beaver were extirpated, common terns (*Sterna hirundo*) were extirpated from Belle Isle, wild celery was substantially reduced in certain areas, no lake sturgeon or lake whitefish were reproducing in the river, and walleye were considered in a crisis state by the Great Lakes Fishery Commission. Today, bald eagles, peregrine falcons, osprey, lake sturgeon, and lake whitefish are reproducing again, beaver are back, common terns are back on Belle Isle, wild celery is thriving, and the Detroit River is now considered part of the "Walleye Capital of the World." This return of the Detroit River's charismatic megafauna and other indicator species represents one of the most remarkable ecological recovery stories in North America (table 5).

Clearly this remarkable recovery is due, in part, to how polluted the river was in the 1960s. However, if the Detroit River can rise like the phoenix from the ashes, from its infamy as a polluted river in the Rust Belt to one of the most remarkable ecological recovery stories in North America, it can be done elsewhere, and this gives hope.

Today, as a result of this ecological recovery, the public perception of the Detroit River is changing. The Detroit River is no longer perceived as a working river that just supports industry and commerce or as a polluted river in the Rust Belt. Today, the Detroit River is the only river system in North America to receive both Canadian Heritage and American Heritage River designations, and the Detroit River and western Lake Erie are now the only international wildlife refuge in North America (i.e., the Detroit River International Wildlife Refuge). These designations have become a major source of community pride.

Out of the convergence of growing public and private support to gain access to the Detroit River, the ecological revival of the river, new designations as an American and Canadian Heritage River, and the establishment of the only international wildlife refuge in North America came an opportunity to reenvision the downtown Detroit waterfront as a gathering place for both people and wildlife. Rising to this challenge would not be easy, but the results were surprising to most people and truly remarkable.

TABLE 5. Evidence of the Return of Sentinel Wildlife Species in the Detroit River Watershed, Representing One of the Most Remarkable Recovery Stories in North America

SPECIES	EVIDENCE OF RECOVERY
Bald Eagle (*Haliaeetus leucocephalus*)	There was nearly complete reproductive failure of the bald eagle population by the mid-1970s. Based on monitoring by the U.S. Fish and Wildlife Service, there has been a steady increase in the number of occupied bald eagle nests per year in metropolitan Detroit since 1991. During 2012–15, twenty-five or more active nests were documented. This nesting success resulted in the fledgling of twenty-eight or more young per year during 2012–15.
Peregrine Falcon (*Falco columbarius*)	The peregrine falcon population was decimated by the 1950s and reintroduced in Detroit in 1987. Since the early 1990s falcon reproductive success has steadily increased, culminating in 1999 when the peregrine falcon was removed from the endangered species list (Yerkey and Payne 2007). Based on monitoring by the Michigan Department of Natural Resources during 2011–16, twenty-two to thirty have been produced per year in southeast Michigan.
Osprey (*Pandion haliaetus*)	A dramatic decline of osprey occurred throughout North America due to widespread use of DDT and other organochlorine pesticides that caused eggshell thinning. In the early 1960s, the osprey population in Michigan was rapidly declining. By 1999 there was only one active nest in southern Michigan. Michigan Osprey, a citizen organization devoted to tracking and restoring the osprey population, has reported that in southeast Michigan alone (i.e., Wayne, Macomb, Oakland, Livingston, Washtenaw, Monroe, and St. Clair counties) there were thirty-eight, fifty, and fifty-two nesting pairs in 2015, 2016, and 2017, respectively.
Common tern (*Sterna hirundo*)	In the 1960s, common tern was extirpated from Belle Isle. The Detroit Zoo and the U.S. Fish and Wildlife Service have reported that from 2012 to 2016, six to twelve pairs of common terns nested on restored Belle Isle habitat per year. In 2016, sixteen chicks were produced from twenty-four active nests.
Lake Sturgeon (*Acipenser fluvescens*)	There was a substantial decline in sturgeon population between the late 1800s and early 1900s. No sturgeon spawning was recorded from the 1970s to 1999. In 2001, sturgeon reproduction was documented for the first time in thirty years. Mark-and-recapture data collected during 2016 have been used to estimate the size of the lake sturgeon population in the Detroit River at 6,360 (95 percent confidence interval: 3,106–13,599 fish) (Chiotti et al. 2012).

Lake Whitefish (*Coregonus clupeaformis*)	In 2006, lake whitefish spawning was documented in the Detroit River for the first time since 1916 (Roseman et al. 2012).
Walleye (*Sander vitreus*)	In the 1970s, the walleye population was considered to be in crisis by the Lake Erie Committee of the Great Lakes Fishery Commission. In 2016, the Lake Erie Committee estimated the size of the west-central walleye population at 30.626 million fish, representing a healthy fishery (Kayle et al. 2015). Today, the Detroit River is considered part of the "Walleye Capital of the World" with annual tournaments offering $500,000 in prize money.
Wild Celery (*Vallisneria americana*)	Based on monitoring of historically important duck feeding locations in the lower Detroit River, wild celery tuber abundance declined 72 percent between 1950–51 and 1984–85, and then increased 200 percent between 1984–85 and 1996–97 (Schloesser and Manny 2007).
Mayflies (*Hexagenia* spp.)	No mayfly larvae were found in the Detroit river during 1929–30 surveys (Wright and Tidd 1933). Riverwide monitoring has documented an increase in mayfly nymph abundance from less than ten nymphs per m^2 in 1968 to twenty or more nymphs per m^2 in 1999 and 2004 (the two most recent years sampled) (Ciborowski 2007). Areas of the river still impacted by pollution continue to show low mayfly larvae abundance (particularly downstream of the confluence of the Rouge River and the Trenton Channel).
American Beaver (*Castor canadensis*)	Beaver were extirpated from the region during the fur trade era. During the height of oil pollution during the 1940s–1970s, beaver could not have survived in the Detroit River because oiled fur becomes matted and they lose their ability to trap air and water to maintain body temperatures. In 2008, beaver returned to the Detroit River for the first time since 1877 (Johnson 1919), representing a 131-year absence. As of 2013, beaver had been reported at six locations in the Detroit River watershed.

CHAPTER 4

Forging the Detroit RiverWalk

t was a dark and dreary day in 1990 that I looked east out a window in the Renaissance Center and saw block after block of dilapidated and abandoned buildings, underutilized street parking lots, material storage piles, and three cement silos dominating the waterfront of the Detroit River in a fashion that prohibited any public access (figures 18–20). For over a century city planners identified the highest and best use of this land to be "industrial" because of the quick and obvious revenue returns. Detroit was an industrial town, and it had a working riverfront that supported industry and commerce. However, times had changed. There were fewer people and industries, and much underutilized and undervalued riverfront land. Detroiters had long lost their connection to the Detroit River, and they wanted to improve public access to it and redevelop it in a fashion that would improve quality of live, catalyze economic development, and help change the perception of Detroit from that of a Rust Belt city to one that is actively engaged in sustainable redevelopment. Simply put, more and more people wanted to overcome

FIGURES 18–20. Material storage piles and dilapidated and abandoned buildings (18), cement silos (19), and underutilized surface parking lots (20) dominating the east riverfront of the Detroit River east of the Renaissance Center, late 1990s.

their historical separation from the river caused by commercial development and to reap the many benefits associated with it. The challenge and stakes were enormous.

It should be noted that there were numerous historical attempts in Detroit to create a more open and accessible riverfront, starting with Detroit mayor Hazen Pingree who, during his four-year term staring in 1889, proposed a plan for an extended park along Detroit's riverfront (Hartig and Wallace 2015). However, all of them failed.

In more recent years it is fair to say that there was no single catalytic moment that created the Detroit RiverWalk. Rather, it was a series of events and initiatives that gradually brought a more publicly accessible and environmentally friendly riverfront dream to reality (table 6). One early initiative was a 1976 study titled *The Land & the River* undertaken by an Interagency Task Force for Detroit/Wayne County Riverfront Development (1976) that inventoried riverfront lands and took stock of future possibilities beyond an industrial waterfront. As a result of that study, the city of Detroit developed a Linked Riverfront Parks Plan in 1979–80 as a blueprint for creation of a system of riverfront parks linked by pedestrian trails. In many respects, that Linked Riverfront Parks Plan was the early foundation upon which today's Detroit RiverWalk is being built.

Another key moment in riverfront history was when the late Peter Stroh, a fourth-generation executive of the Stroh Brewing Company in Detroit, purchased the former world headquarters of Parke, Davis & Company in 1979 for mixed-use redevelopment as Stroh River Place. The Stroh River Place campus includes fifteen separate buildings that were converted into offices, retail, and housing. The flagship of the Stroh River Place campus is 300 River Place, a 500,000-square-foot, multitenant general office and retail building that includes one of Detroit's premier restaurants called the Rattlesnake Club. This clearly was instrumental in laying the foundation for the Detroit RiverWalk and provided an early example of the unique role of business. Other planning initiatives

TABLE 6. A Chronology of Major Events or Initiatives That Helped Lay the Foundation for and Create the Detroit RiverWalk

DATE	MAJOR EVENT OR INITIATIVE
1976	Publication of a report titled *The Land & the River* by an Interagency Task Force for Detroit/Wayne County Riverfront Development (1976); this study inventoried riverfront lands and took stock of future possibilities beyond an industrial waterfront
1979	Former World Headquarters of Parke, Davis & Company purchased by the Stroh Companies for mixed-use redevelopment along the Detroit riverfront
1979–80	Linked Riverfront Parks Plan developed by city of Detroit
1982	The city of Detroit convened a conference on "The Riverfront as a Resource: Programming for Today and Tomorrow" that explored recreational use of the riverfront
1982	Chene Park completed as a music and entertainment venue that would attract people to the riverfront; it also was constructed in direct support of Detroit's Linked Riverfront Parks Plan
early-1980s	St. Aubin Marina constructed as one of the few public watercraft harbors along the Detroit River; it also was constructed in direct support of Detroit's Linked Riverfront Parks Plan
1989	Michigan Rails-to-Trails office opened to catalyze greenways across Michigan
1990	Southeast Michigan Greenways Initiative established to champion greenways
1998	Greater Detroit American Heritage River Initiative established; linked riverfront greenways identified as one of the five program priorities
1999	Publication of a report titled *Detroit's New Front Porch: A Riverfront Greenway in Southwest Detroit* that helped catalyze riverfront greenways (Cox 1999)
2001	Detroit celebrated its 300th anniversary of its founding in 1701; award-winning Campus Martius Park restored as the legacy project of Detroit 300; Underground Railroad Monument placed on the riverfront; greenways championed through year-long celebration
2001	General Motors completed a $500 million renovation of its world headquarters (called the Renaissance Center) on the Detroit riverfront that included a new five-story glass atrium that represented a new front door on the Detroit River
2001	Community Foundation for Southeast Michigan launched its Greenways Initiative that raised $25 million to be given away in grants to communities to help make match requirements on federal and state greenways grants

2001	United Auto Workers and General Motors opened a 65,000-square-foot education and training center on the Detroit riverfront called the UAW-GM Training Center
2002	Blue Ribbon Committee established by the mayor of Detroit to articulate a vision for transforming the Detroit riverfront; the vision included 5.5 miles of greenways from the Ambassador Bridge (linking to Canada) to the MacArthur Bridge (linking to Belle Isle, a 982-acre island park in the Detroit River)
2002	The Kresge Foundation committed $50 million, the largest gift in the history of the foundation, to create the Detroit RiverWalk
2003	Detroit RiverFront Conservancy established to improve, operate, maintain, secure, and program the Detroit RiverWalk; Faye Nelson hired as president and chief executive officer of the Detroit RiverFront Conservancy
2004	St. Aubin Park and Marina transferred from Detroit Parks and Recreation Department to the Michigan Department of Natural Resources and renamed Tri-Centennial State Park, creating the first state park in Detroit and committing resources to help support the Detroit RiverWalk
2007	Detroit Greenways Coalition established
2009	Tri-Centennial State Park renamed Milliken State Park in honor of former Michigan governor William Milliken; continued state investment in this riverfront state park
2009	First phase of Dequindre Cut Greenway opens, linking the RiverWalk with Eastern Market
2011	New $25.1 million Detroit/Wayne County Port Authority facility opened on the Detroit RiverWalk, complete with a cruise ship (up to five-hundred-foot vessels) dock to welcome tourists
2013	Presbyterian Villages of Michigan, United Methodist Retirement Communities, and the Henry Ford Health System open a $35 million senior living complex adjacent to the Detroit RiverWalk
2013	Detroit leases Belle Isle, the terminus of the Detroit RiverWalk, to the Michigan Department of Natural Resources for thirty years; this brought in $10–20 million in new revenue for park upgrades in the first three years of the lease
2013	Detroit RiverFront Conservancy celebrated its ten-year anniversary, representing over $1 billion of public and private investment along the riverfront in the first ten years and the creation of 16,700 jobs
2014	Mark Wallace hired as president and chief executive officer of the Detroit RiverFront Conservancy

2015	Michigan Department of Natural Resources opened a new 43,000-square-foot Outdoor Adventure Center in the former Globe Trading Company building adjacent to Milliken State Park that at one time was the home of the Detroit Shipbuilding Company and the place where the young Henry Ford apprenticed
2015	West Riverfront Park (now Ralph C. Wilson, Jr. Centennial Park) opens
2016	Work to connect the RiverWalk from Stroh River Place to Chene Park East begins
2016	C. David Campbell Memorial Terrace opens on the Dequindre Cut as a small-scale outdoor performance space
2017	Detroit RiverFront Conservancy, city of Detroit, and Detroit Economic Growth Corporation announce new plan to preserve and expand riverfront access; design process begins for Ralph C. Wilson, Jr. Centennial Park (formerly West Riverfront Park)
2017	Orleans Landing opens on the RiverWalk as a mixed-use community with 278 market-rate apartments; fifty-six of the units are set aside to be affordable to residents earning up to 80 percent of the area median income
2017	Twenty-six-mile inner circle greenway named Joe Louis Greenway
2018	Groundbreaking on Atwater Beach, a new sand beach and play area for families that will include a floating barge for food and drinks

were undertaken over time that built momentum. Then in 2001 four significant things happened that would provide another foretaste of a future riverfront greenway:

- General Motors completed a $500 million renovation of its world headquarters (called the Renaissance Center) and switched the building front door from Jefferson Avenue (facing inland) to one facing the Detroit River with the construction of a five-story glass atrium called the Wintergarden
- Community Foundation for Southeast Michigan launched its Greenways Initiative that had raised $25 million to be given away in grants to communities to help make match requirements on federal and state greenways grants
- United Auto Workers and General Motors opened a 65,000-

square-foot education and training center on the Detroit riverfront
called the UAW-GM Training Center

- Detroit celebrated its 300th anniversary that included restoration
  of Campus Martius Park as its legacy project of Detroit 300
  and placement of an Underground Railroad Monument on the
  riverfront.

Together, these four significant developments gave further traction to the
desire for a connected riverfront greenway and gave confidence to the city
of Detroit to bring key stakeholders together to create an organization
that would lead the effort.

City of Detroit Appoints a Blue Ribbon Committee
to Transform the Detroit Riverfront

Based on past experiences with riverfront planning, the city of Detroit
wanted to make sure that any new vision and plan for the riverfront had
the support of a broad diversity of the people living in the Detroit area
and the many stakeholder groups that would impact or be impacted
by a transformed riverfront. In 2002, Detroit mayor Kwame Kilpatrick
assembled an East Riverfront Study Group made up of thirty-four people
representing a broad range of interests and charged them with developing
a revitalization strategy for Detroit's east riverfront. Organizers did not
want a protracted planning process, so they commissioned the group to
report back in ninety days. The study group was cochaired by Derrick
Miller, chief administrative officer of the city of Detroit, and Matthew
Cullen, general manager of Economic Development and Enterprise
Services for General Motors at that time. The designation of these
cochairs sent a clear message that this effort would be a public–private
partnership. Other members of the study group included other city
departments, Wayne County government, state government, federal
government, nongovernmental organizations, corporations, foundations

like the Kresge Foundation , the Community Foundation for Southeast Michigan, and the McGregor Fund, and community groups.

The first task at hand was to reach agreement on a compelling vision for a revitalized riverfront. After much input and debate, the following vision was agreed to:

> The historic Detroit River is a gathering place for Detroiters, their families, friends, and visitors—a place where people want to live, work, and play. The riverfront illustrates our ability to provide stewardship of our environment, confirms our ability to connect and care for our people and channels sustainable economic development for the benefit of all. Our riverfront is transformed and we are recognized as an outstanding global community. (Hemming 2005, 398)

From the outset it was understood that no single organization or entity could do this alone. To manifest this, study group members each signed an agreement that every participant would do everything within their power to bring this vision to reality (Hemming 2005).

That same year in 2002, the Kresge Foundation committed $50 million in a series of challenge grants over a five-year period to help build the Detroit RiverWalk, the largest gift in the history of the foundation at that time (Hemming 2005). The Kresge Foundation had its roots in Detroit and wanted to give this transformational project and its stakeholders momentum. The foundation also stipulated that an endowment would be created to ensure long-term, quality operation, maintenance, and programming.

Creation of the Detroit RiverFront Conservancy

In direct response to the work of the city of Detroit's East Riverfront Study Group, the $50 million commitment of the Kresge Foundation, and the support of General Motors Corporation, the Detroit RiverFront

Conservancy, Inc. was formed in 2003 as a 501(c)(3), nonprofit organization with the mission of developing public access to Detroit's riverfront and to have this development serve as an anchor for economic revitalization—all while working with others to create a more thriving, walkable, and connected community within Detroit.

The vision was for a riverfront greenway extending 5.5 miles from the MacArthur Bridge that connects to Belle Isle to the Ambassador Bridge that connects to Canada. The Detroit RiverFront Conservancy would build the Detroit RiverWalk, including all plazas, pavilions, and green spaces, and was given the responsibility for the improvement, operations, maintenance, and programming of the RiverWalk, in perpetuity.

The bylaws of the Detroit RiverFront Conservancy called for a board of directors that represented a broad range of public and private interests considered critical to the success of the Detroit RiverWalk. In total, forty-four members were appointed, including business, labor, city, county, state, and federal governments, private property owners, community groups, and tourism and economic development organizations. Eight committees were initially struck, including Executive, Audit, Advancement and Membership, Community Outreach and Communications, Finance and Investment, Governance and Nominating, Operations and Programming, and Planning, Design, and Development. The board appointed Matthew Cullen and Derrick Miller to serve as cochairpersons, and David Page as vice chairperson, who at the time was vice chairperson of the Kresge Foundation and a senior partner in the Detroit law firm of Honigman Miller Schwartz and Cohn, LLP. Also in 2003, the board hired Faye Alexander Nelson as president and chief executive officer of the Detroit RiverFront Conservancy. In total, over one hundred influential and highly committed individuals were actively involved in the work of the board and its committees. All had a sense of urgency to bring the Detroit RiverWalk vision to reality.

"When we started this process, we identified non-negotiables to getting the job done: the vision to make it happen; the money to make it happen; the will to make it happen; and the people to make it happen.

We now have all of those in place," noted Matthew Cullen. "Detroit's riverfront will make an unparalleled contribution to the image of Detroit as a destination, as our home, as a host to global reaching events like Super Bowl XL, the NCAA Final Four basketball tournament, and Major League Baseball's All Star Game."

At the outset, the board of directors reached agreement on a set of principles that would guide decision-making for the RiverWalk (table 7). These principles were developed to help ensure that the RiverWalk would be accessible, safe, and well-maintained, create connections, celebrate history and culture, promote mixed-use redevelopment and sustainable economic development, reconnect people with nature, and evoke a sense of stewardship.

The Detroit RiverWalk Becomes a Reality

From the very outset the plan was to build the Detroit RiverWalk from the MacArthur Bridge on the east to the Ambassador Bridge on the west. For practical reasons, the RiverWalk project had to be broken up into phases. The first phase was called the East Riverfront and extended from the MacArthur Bridge to Joe Louis Arena, a distance of about 3.5 miles. The second phase was called the West Riverfront and extended from Joe Louis Arena to the Ambassador Bridge, a distance of about two miles.

The Detroit RiverFront Conservancy hired the Smith Group, a national architecture, engineering, and planning firm from Detroit, to serve as the lead architect for the RiverWalk. Included on their design team were many other firms: Wade Trim, Inc.; Somat Engineering; NTH Consultants; Hines; Tucker, Young, Jackson, and Tull, Inc.; Greenburg Consultants; Madison & Madison; Brinker; Giffels Webster; Multi-Solutions; and others. The team included experienced international experts and the best and the brightest local talent.

Substantial efforts were made to ensure that there was an inclusive

TABLE 7. A Set of Principles Developed and Endorsed to Guide Decision Making for Creating and Maintaining the Detroit RiverWalk

PRINCIPLE	DESCRIPTION
Build on the Unique Urban and Natural Assets of the Riverfront	• Reconnection between people and nature • Link riverfront to key areas via greenways • Natural environment in urban space • Active and passive activities, stewardship for a vibrant, healthy community
Provide Optimal Connectivity and Access	• Balanced network of streets • Public links from Jefferson Avenue to water's edge • Promenade along riverfront • Comprehensive parking strategy • New Port Authority Terminal
Guarantee Economic Growth Through a Results-Driven Process	• Framework to foster diverse housing options • District for sustainable phased economic development • Plan that promotes mixed-use development • Enduring and unique sense of place, competitive advantage • Robust planning that leads to expedited development
Leverage and Enhance Historic Resources	• Memorable civic waterfront combining elements (e.g., river heritage, ribbon farms, music, automobile history, sports, commerce) • Preserve/adapt rich legacy of historical resources for new uses • Celebrate unique culture and heritage • Reemphasize international border • Leverage Greater Detroit American Heritage River Initiative and Automobile National Heritage Area
Evoke a Sense of Place	• East riverfront home to Detroit's newest neighborhoods • Unique physical qualities of riverfront to define its character • Vibrant district, pedestrian friendly, street-level destination and activities • Safe, secure, well-maintained, family-friendly environment • Create special places, that make connections between buildings and gathering places, accessible • Revitalize and unify district, complementary architectural themes and materials

planning process, one where all voices were heard and factored in. For example, the vision was presented and stakeholder input obtained in nearly one hundred meetings attended by over four thousand people (Hemming 2005). Public interest was high, and some of the community design workshops attracted over six hundred people. The most frequent stakeholder concerns received included the need to address transportation/access problems, retaining the historical heritage of Detroit, ensuring safety and cleanliness, and ensuring meaningful involvement of the local community.

Detroit RiverFront Conservancy staff and the board of directors worked hard to address all concerns and move forward with a sense of urgency to build the RiverWalk. In addition to providing residents and visitors with a beautiful and safe place to walk, jog, and ride a bicycle, the Detroit RiverFront Conservancy placed a priority on catalyzing economic development. Throughout the entire process, the conservancy goal was to develop a collective sense of ownership, accessibility, and responsibility; enhance Detroit's image to emphasize its iconic, international riverfront; and create and maintain an inviting destination for all. Clearly, there were obstacles to reclaiming this waterfront as a destination for all. One example was that three cement silos dominated 12.5 acres of the east riverfront. The city of Detroit, the Detroit Economic Growth Corporation, the Detroit RiverFront Conservancy, and others worked to relocate these cement operations to a more appropriate industrial area downstream, acquired the land, demolished the existing silos, and cleaned up the land to become part of the RiverWalk and a state park. The land transactions and cleanup efforts took several years, concluding in 2006.

Another potential obstacle was casinos. In 1996 a statewide ballot initiative passed, granting three casinos in Detroit. From the outset there was a push to locate these gambling casinos on Detroit's east riverfront. Considerable public outcry followed, stating that locating casinos on the riverfront was not the highest and best use of this land. This public debate continued for nearly ten years. Following this considerable public outcry, it was finally determined that these three casinos would be located inland and not on the waterfront. The city of Detroit, with considerable support from many stakeholder groups, finally concluded that providing public access to the waterfront was paramount.

The establishment of the Detroit RiverFront Conservancy in 2003 captured this public sentiment that the riverfront should be a destination for all. An aggressive development program was undertaken to raise the necessary funds to build, operate, maintain, and program the Detroit RiverWalk. The projected cost of building the East Riverfront portion of the Detroit RiverWalk alone was $140 million. In its first ten years of existence, the Detroit RiverFront Conservancy raised over $110 million. In addition, a $60 million endowment target was set to ensure long-term operation, maintenance, and programming, in perpetuity. By the end of its first ten years, the Detroit RiverFront Conservancy had $42 million invested in its endowment.

Presented below are selected examples of how the Detroit RiverWalk is being built as a necklace, with the strand of the necklace being the RiverWalk and the beads being unique destinations for commerce, recreation, and entertainment, consistent with the 2002 vision and guiding principles identified in table 7.

Gabriel Richard Park

This beloved Detroit park is located just east of the MacArthur Bridge to Belle Isle. It is named after Father Gabriel Richard who was an important pastor, educator, and public servant. He came to Detroit in 1797 as the assistant pastor of Ste. Anne's Church. Though his calling was missionary work, he brought the first printing press to Michigan, publishing a grammar textbook for children as his first document. He established schools for Native Americans and women and was elected a nonvoting

DETROIT RIVERFRONT CONSERVANCY

FIGURE 21. Gabriel Richard Park that serves as the easternmost anchor of the Detroit RiverWalk.

delegate of the Michigan Territory to the U.S. House of Representatives for the Eighteenth Congress (1823–25). In 1805 a fire nearly destroyed the entire city. As a result of that tragedy, Father Richard wrote Detroit's motto: "We hope for better days; it will arise from the ashes."

Today, Father Richard would be so proud of the park named in his honor that has become the eastern anchor of the Detroit RiverWalk (figure 21). It is a beautiful and serene oasis that features lush landscaping, a whimsical fountain for children to play in, butterfly gardens, a soft-engineered shoreline that enhances aquatic habitat, a contemplative labyrinth, an entry-level birding spot, fishing outlooks, and restroom facilities. More recent improvements have included installing an environmentally friendly parking lot and pathways to better link the park with Jefferson Avenue and tasteful lighting to better illuminate the popular labyrinth.

Gabriel Richard Park also has an awesome plaza and pavilion that make a perfect spot to relax, watch the river flow by, and view Belle Isle. It is an ideal spot for a day of outdoor fun, recreation, and relaxation.

LEO WEISSBURG

FIGURE 22. Mt. Elliott Park that features a schooner-themed, interactive water park.

Mt. Elliott Park

If you were going to build something of public interest next to a U.S. Coast Guard Station and the oldest lighthouse supply depot in the Great Lakes, what would it be? The Detroit RiverFront Conservancy provided the answer when it transformed Mt. Elliott Park into a sunken, schooner-themed, interactive water park, complete with water jets and cannons. Water actually cascades out of the mast of a Great Lakes schooner and shoots up out of the ground. This nautical theme park blends perfectly with adjacent Coast Guard cutters and Detroit's unique piece of maritime history that was built in the late 1800s as a warehouse for the storage of wicks, oil, lamps, buoys, and accoutrements that were needed to maintain lighthouses.

Transformation of Mt. Elliott Park into a maritime playground for the young and young-at-heart was completed in 2013 (figure 22). Mt. Elliott Park is located at the foot of Mt. Elliott Street along the Detroit

RiverWalk. It has numerous family-friendly amenities in addition to the sunken, schooner-themed water park, including an open-air pavilion where you can have lunch or a snack, a playscape with drum seats and sound chimes, fishing outlooks, and colorful landscaping. With child-activated water cannons, it is the perfect place to cool off on a hot summer day. Water cascades out of the schooner mast and shoots up out of the ground. It is also universally accessible, meaning it is accessible to all children and adults, including those with disabilities. If you are looking for a place to encourage imagination and entertain your children, then Mt. Elliott Park is a must stop.

UAW-GM Center for Human Resources

Sitting on the banks of the Detroit River just west of Mt. Elliott Park is the largest industrial training center in North America. It was opened by the United Auto Workers-General Motors (UAW-GM) Center for Human Resources in 2001. This state-of-the-art, sixteen-acre training center serves as the national headquarters for UAW-GM joint programs and activities focused on health and safety, training and skill development, employee educational opportunities, work and family support, and product quality. It consolidated operations previously housed in three separate locations.

The complex is anchored by a seven-story office tower, with an adjacent three-story training center and four-hundred-seat auditorium (figure 23). As part of UAW-GM's commitment to riverfront revitalization, they built nine hundred feet of riverfront greenway that is now part of the RiverWalk, representing one of the first private organizations to develop public space along the riverfront.

LEO WEISSBURG

FIGURE 23. The UAW-GM Center for Human Resources provided nine hundred feet of public riverfront greenway as part of its commitment to riverfront revitalization.

SMITH-GROUP/JJR

FIGURE 24. The Stroh River Place campus with a cantilevered section of the Detroit RiverWalk built out over the Detroit River.

Stroh River Place and Talon Center

As noted earlier, Stroh River Place is a twenty-five-acre mixed-use campus located on the RiverWalk that brings together the best in business amenities and upscale living. The campus includes 300 River Place, a 500,000-square-foot, multitenant general office and retail building, one of Detroit's premier restaurants called the Rattlesnake Club, Talon Office Center, Roberts Riverwalk Hotel, an athletic club, and more.

Land for the public RiverWalk was limited, so the Detroit RiverFront Conservancy's team worked with Stroh Companies to build a one-thousand-foot, cantilevered walkway out over the water in 2006–7, creating a win-win for both the private and public interests (figure 24). In addition, beneath the cantilevered RiverWalk, the team restored fish habitat in support of the ecological recovery of the Detroit River.

Chene Park

Cars may be Detroit's main export commodity, but music runs a close second. Whether it's rock and roll, Motown, jazz, rhythm and blues, funk, hip-hop, or classical, Detroit's rich music tradition has impacted the world. Located along the Detroit RiverWalk and overlooking the Detroit River is an outdoor amphitheater that brings thousands of visitors to the waterfront during the warm weather months to hear legendary artists and high-profile entertainers. Built in 1982, Chene Park is an extraordinary, outdoor entertainment venue that is second to none. This six-thousand-person amphitheater has five thousand seats and one thousand lawn spaces offering exceptional, live, outdoor concerts with an unequalled view of the Detroit River and Canada (figure 25). Chene Park also includes trails, the Chene Park Fountain, and the Lake Lounge Bar. Pollstar (2017), a trade publication that covers the worldwide concert industry, has rated Chene Park as one of the top one hundred concert venues in the world.

CHENE PARK DETROIT

FIGURE 25. Chene Park Amphitheater overlooking the Detroit River and Canada.

Dequindre Cut Greenway

The Dequindre Cut Greenway is a unique, 1.5-mile, nonmotorized trail that initially connected the Detroit RiverWalk to Eastern Market and several residential neighborhoods in between (figure 26). It was originally built as a Grand Trunk Railroad line that was predominately below street level running between Gratiot Avenue and Atwater Street, and parallel to St. Aubin Street. This greenway trail was completed in 2009 using a unique partnership that included the federal government, the city of Detroit, the Community Foundation for Southeast Michigan, the Detroit Economic Growth Corporation, and the Detroit RiverFront Conservancy.

Well known for its unique urban artwork and graffiti, the Dequindre Cut Greenway features a twenty-foot-wide paved pathway that has

FIGURE 26. The Dequindre Cut Greenway that links the Detroit RiverWalk with Eastern Market and several residential neighborhoods.

separate lanes for pedestrian and bicycle traffic. Entrance ramps to the cut are located at Atwater Street, Franklin Street, Lafayette Street, Gratiot Avenue, and Woodbridge Street. Strategically located just west of the foot of the Dequindre Cut Greenway is a bicycle livery called Wheelhouse Detroit for bicycle rentals, sales, and repairs.

The Dequindre Cut Greenway was later extended one half mile north from Gratiot Avenue to Mack Avenue and now links to the 3.5-mile Midtown Loop and many cultural attractions. This means that residents and visitors can now walk or bike from the RiverWalk, through Eastern Market (a farmers' market established in 1891 that is frequented by some forty-five thousand people each Saturday), and to Midtown, Wayne State University, and Hamtramck. Eventually, it will connect to the twenty-six-mile Joe Louis Greenway that is designed to connect city neighborhoods and residents to Detroit assets like parks, commercial corridors, the RiverWalk, and downtown. The Inner Circle Greenway is projected to be completed in 2019.

SMITHGROUPJJR

FIGURE 27. Innovative stormwater treatment system constructed in Milliken State Park.

Milliken State Park

Those not from Detroit might not realize that Milliken State Park and Harbor is the first urban state park in Michigan. It is replete with a fifty-two-slip harbor for boats, wetlands, "Anglers Avenue" for fishing, a portion of the RiverWalk, and lighthouse. It is located on the riverfront, bordered by Orleans and St. Aubin Roads and quickly becoming a go-to destination in the city. It has been described as a thirty-one-acre green oasis carved out on the banks of the Detroit River in the middle of Michigan's largest city.

Milliken State Park boasts a sixty-three-foot tall lighthouse that is modeled after the historic light towers that once dotted the Detroit River. It is also nearly a full-scale model of the tower at Tawas Point Lighthouse in Michigan's northeastern Lower Peninsula. The park also hosts an annual kids free fishing day that attracts four hundred or more children to learn the basics of fishing, while creating lasting memories and enjoying the beautiful Detroit River. Program highlights include fishing instruction from expert anglers, free food and prizes, face painting, arts and crafts, and a kids' fun zone. Key sponsors of the event include Rivertown Detroit Association, Michigan Department of Natural Resources, U.S. Fish and Wildlife Service, Detroit RiverFront Conservancy, and others.

One innovative element of Milliken State Park is its urban stormwater management system (figure 27). Stormwater management is one of Detroit's biggest challenges, and nowhere is treatment showcased better. Milliken State Park has constructed an innovative urban stormwater treatment system that collects runoff from adjacent lands and treats it naturally before discharging it into the Detroit River. Benefits of this urban stormwater treatment system include:

- filtering an estimated 4.5 million gallons of stormwater runoff annually from 12.5 acres of developable properties adjacent to the park (removing an estimated 99 percent of sediment, 91 percent of phosphorus, 74 percent of nitrogen, 97 percent of lead, 91 percent of copper, and 87 percent of zinc from surface runoff from surrounding parcels);
- creating native habitat for sixty-two species of migratory and resident birds (e.g., Virginia rails, red-winged blackbirds, swamp sparrows, and marsh wrens), which were not present on the previous brownfield, as well as species of reptiles and amphibians such as bullfrogs, green frogs, and painted turtles;
- sequestering three tons of carbon per year in over 450 trees and shrubs on the once largely unvegetated site;
- providing a space for outdoor recreation, exercise, and relaxation for a projected one million annual visitors, including eleven thousand employees working within 0.25 mile of the site at the Renaissance Center;
- providing educational opportunities for more than 1,641 visitors

through the Michigan Department of Natural Resources Explorer Program in 2012;

- connecting 3.5 miles of the Detroit RiverWalk to the eastern trailhead of the 1.5 mile long Dequindre Cut trail that extends from the river westward to the popular Eastern Market and Midtown residential districts, enhancing nonmotorized circulation and providing linkages to other existing and proposed trail networks in the city;
- generating a projected $5.82 million annually in economic activity from visitors' spending; and
- catalyzing a projected $152.3 million in multifamily residential development within the site's watershed.

Outdoor Adventure Center

While it is not always apparent that nature can be found in major cities, the Michigan Department of Natural Resources and many partners opened an Outdoor Adventure Center in 2014 to showcase the best of Michigan's natural resources and outdoor recreation to visitors interested in learning more about the abundant outdoor recreational opportunities available in the Great Lakes state (figure 28). This Outdoor Adventure Center is located on the Detroit RiverWalk at the beginning of the Dequindre Cut Greenway, which makes it a superb location for walkers, joggers, and bikers who avail themselves of this new recreational jewel. Further, it is located immediately across the street from Milliken State Park, creating a unique recreational synergy and a go-to destination for both residents and visitors alike. Over one hundred thousand visitors came to the center in its first two years to experience Michigan's great outdoors in the heart of the city. It is projected that as many as one million annual visitors will come to the center.

The center is an adaptive reuse of the former Globe Building, also

FIGURE 28. Michigan Department of Natural Resources' Outdoor Adventure Center located at the intersection of the Detroit RiverWalk and the Dequindre Cut Greenway, and right across from Milliken State Park.

known by its earlier name Detroit Dry Dock Engine Works that dates to the late nineteenth century when it served as a maintenance yard for Great Lakes shipping. The building is also notable for its innovative steel-frame structure and its connection to a young Henry Ford, who apprenticed there as a machinist.

Indeed, Henry Ford, who was an environmentalist before it was fashionable, would be so pleased with this Outdoor Adventure Center. The center is not just a place to look and learn, but an opportunity for anyone to enjoy a firsthand experience to fish, shoot a bow and arrow, put up a tent, stand in an eagle nest, crawl through a beaver dam, or see an unfettered view of the night sky as if standing in the middle of a state park in the wilderness. It provides an opportunity for those who haven't truly experienced the Michigan outdoors to do so. It is a hands-on museum, exhibit and training center, classroom, and student laboratory all rolled into one. The Outdoor Adventure Center can also be rented out for weddings, birthday parties, and corporate events. It truly is a must-see for both visitors and residents alike.

This $12.8 million center houses hands-on simulators that introduce visitors to various outdoor recreational experiences and has exhibits and displays that showcase the natural and cultural resources found in Michigan in state parks, recreation areas, beaches, trails, and harbors. For both the young and young at heart, the center has a climbing wall; kayaking, snowmobiling, off-road vehicle riding, and bicycling simulators; and science classrooms. "Our goal is to really bring the outdoors indoors," noted Vicki McGhee-Anthes, chief of the Planning Section of the Michigan Department of Natural Resources' Parks and Recreation Division.

Cullen Plaza

Cullen Plaza is located about one-quarter mile east of the Renaissance Center and has become one of the east riverfront's most popular, family-friendly destinations (figure 29). It is a destination that landscape architects call urban picturesque because of the compelling pedestrian experience provided within an aesthetically pleasing, natural, urban landscape. Compelling views of the Detroit River, Belle Isle, the Windsor waterfront, the Renaissance Center, and the Ambassador Bridge to Canada greet you everywhere you turn. One show-stopping attraction is the handcrafted Cullen Family Carousel that features creatures native to the Detroit River, including lake sturgeon, egrets, walleye, and even a mythical river mermaid and river monster. Other key attractions include an inlaid granite map of the Detroit River, a standing glass sculptured map of the St. Lawrence Seaway, a children's playscape, playful fountains, and lush landscaping.

If you are hungry, Cullen Plaza offers the tantalizing creations of the RiverWalk Café. After work you can enjoy your favorite wine or

DETROIT RIVERFRONT CONSERVANCY

FIGURE 29. Cullen Plaza, a destination of choice along the Detroit RiverWalk one-quarter mile east of the Renaissance Center.

beer overlooking the Detroit River. If you want to ride a bike, go on a bicycle tour, purchase a bike, or get one repaired, Cullen Plaza features Wheelhouse Detroit. Also, the popular Diamond Jack's River Tours operate out of Cullen Plaza for public boat tours on the Detroit River or for private charters. The pavilion building at Cullen Plaza houses public restroom facilities, as well as the Detroit RiverFront Conservancy's operations offices and the security command center. Without a doubt, Cullen Plaza is a must-see destination for all.

GM Wintergarden and Plaza

The Renaissance Center has been a Detroit icon since 1977 and is an office/retail/hotel complex that is one of Detroit's major attractions with

KEN COBB

FIGURE 30. Fountains in the General Motors Plaza in front of their world headquarters in Detroit, Michigan.

more than one million visitors annually. It is a group of seven interconnected skyscrapers in downtown Detroit along the Detroit River. There are four thirty-nine-floor office towers, a central, seventy-three-story, 1,328-room hotel, and two twenty-one-story adjacent office towers that are all right on the Detroit RiverWalk.

In redeveloping the Renaissance Center as its world headquarters, General Motors Corporation turned its front door from facing inland toward Jefferson Avenue to facing the Detroit River. As part of a $500 million redevelopment project, General Motors built a five-story, glass-enclosed, public hall called the Wintergarden in 2001. The Wintergarden provides magnificent views of the Detroit River and Windsor, Ontario, and represents a new front door of its world headquarters facing the Detroit River. The Wintergarden is flanked by two stories of retail space, with additional retail shops and an outdoor restaurant lining the riverfront promenade. It has rapidly become a popular riverfront gathering spot and signature event venue. As part of this redevelopment, General Motors also built a three-thousand-foot riverfront promenade to become part of the Detroit RiverWalk. The Ren Cen has also received Wildlife Habitat Council certification for its work in environmental stewardship and conservation, including a butterfly garden, a rooftop garden and wildlife habitat, bird-watching stations, pollinator habitat, and several monarch butterfly way stations.

Located in the riverfront promenade are fountains that are a focal point for fun and frolic for kids both young and old to play in during the warm summer months (figure 30). Within the Renaissance Center you can enjoy fine dining at some of Detroit's best restaurants or catch a movie at the Ren Cen Theatre. There is something for everyone. As part of its commitment to creating a publically accessible riverfront, General Motors generously donated the first one-half mile of the RiverWalk to the Detroit RiverFront Conservancy.

Detroit/Wayne County Port Authority Building

Most major waterfront cities have docking facilities for domestic and international cruise ships, ferries, tall ships, and other vessels of interest. However, Detroit long lost its capability to welcome such vessels and reap the economic benefits. That all changed in 2011 when the Detroit/ Wayne County Port Authority opened a new $25.1 million public dock and terminal facility on the Detroit River and adjacent to the Detroit RiverWalk (figure 31). It is located at the corner of Atwater and Bates Streets

DETROIT/WAYNE COUNTY PORT AUTHORITY

FIGURE 31. Public dock and terminal facility of the Detroit/Wayne County Port Authority along the Detroit RiverWalk.

in a strategic location between the Renaissance Center and Detroit's Hart Plaza. The public wharf can accommodate a variety of vessels, including cruise ships and naval frigates up to five hundred feet in length.

The 21,000-square-foot facility houses the offices for the Detroit/ Wayne County Port Authority, meeting rooms with a view of the Detroit River, a command room for ships, and state-of-the-art maritime technology to regulate the flow of visitors and ship traffic. The contemporary, glass-facade terminal building was designed for flexibility. It is a two-story structure that includes a customs processing area for visitors, passengers, and tourists from foreign ports on the lower level, and public lounge, open-air balcony, and the administrative offices of the Port Authority on the upper level. Also, the building is open for public use by residents of Detroit, Wayne County, and neighboring communities for special events, gallery exhibits, and business conferences.

This public dock and terminal facility was strategically located on the

Detroit RiverWalk to welcome tourists and offer pedestrian connections to the many attractions along the riverfront. In 2012, the first year the Port Authority facility was open, it hosted thirty-three dinner vessel visits, twelve Great Lakes cruise ship calls, six tall ship visits, and two U.S. Navy ships for a week. This public dock and passenger building also provided commuter ferry service to Belle Isle during the 2012 Detroit Grand Prix that attracted over ninety-five thousand people in a weekend.

One good example of a cruise ship visit to Detroit in 2012 was the *Yorktown Clipper* that brought over two thousand people into downtown Detroit for shoreside excursions to the Henry Ford Museum, Detroit Institute of Arts, and other cultural amenities. It is interesting to note that the *Yorktown Clipper* has designated Detroit as its homeport of choice because of the new public dock and terminal facility and its proximity to Detroit Metropolitan Airport. Passengers typically spend one to two nights in Detroit before continuing on their cruise that includes other Great Lakes port cities. This brings in tourist revenue and supports the local economy. In 2018 Victory Cruise Lines made twenty stops at this Detroit facility and is scheduled to make more than thirty in 2019.

At one time in the 1800s, before there was any bridge or tunnel to Canada, there were over one hundred ferries that would transport people and goods between Detroit and Windsor. The Port Authority is not only bringing cruise ships to downtown Detroit but also wants to eventually reinstate a ferry service across the Detroit River to provide transportation options for the approximately five to six thousand Canadian commuters who work in the health care field and automotive companies in Detroit, and to promote daytrip and bicycle tourism. It is also envisioned to someday offer this ferry service to other communities up and down the Detroit River like Wyandotte, Trenton, and Amherstburg, and even beyond.

ERANDON NAGY

FIGURE 32. Movement Electronic Music Festival at Detroit's Hart Plaza along the Detroit RiverWalk, 2017.

Hart Plaza

Most major cities have a centralized venue for festivals, concerts, and special events. In Detroit, it is called Hart Plaza. Hart Plaza is strategically located at the foot of Woodward Avenue in what most people say is the heart of the Detroit RiverWalk. It is a unique, fourteen-acre, riverfront destination that has two open-air amphitheaters for concerts and plenty of space for festivals that are held May through September. Three good examples of festivals held each year at Hart Plaza include the Detroit Jazz Festival that attracted nearly three hundred thousand people in 2016, the Motor City Pride Concert that attracted over forty thousand in 2017, and the Movement Electronic Music Festival that attracted over one hundred thousand people in 2017 (figure 32). In many respects, Detroit is synonymous with jazz, and to no surprise its Detroit Jazz Festival held at Hart Plaza is the largest free jazz festival in the world. It was founded in 1980 to bring people into the city and to provide all segments of the population with world-class entertainment. It quickly became a Labor Day weekend tradition at Hart Plaza.

Hart Plaza opened in 1975 and has a daily capacity of forty thousand people. It was named after the late U.S. senator Philip Hart who had a distinguished eighteen-year career representing Michigan. At the center of the plaza is the famed Horace E. Dodge and Son Memorial Fountain and *Pylon* art sculpture, designed by Isamu Noguchi in 1978. Other key features include the Underground Railroad Monument and the *Transcending* art sculpture that celebrates Michigan's contributions to the labor movement. There is no doubt that this is a key destination of choice along the Detroit RiverWalk for both entertainment and celebration of history and culture.

Cobo Center

Cobo Hall and Arena first opened in 1960, expanded in 1989, and was renovated in 2015. It is probably best known as the long-standing home of the North American International Auto Show and the home of the Detroit Pistons from 1961 to 1978. It is now called the Cobo Center. A five-year, three-phase renovation was completed in 2015 costing $279 million. These renovations created a new front door on the Detroit River and the Detroit RiverWalk, and made it one of the largest convention sites in the United States (figure 33). The facility hosts events about 320 days a year, including the two-week-long North American International Auto Show each January. Daily attendance at the auto show can reach one hundred thousand. Other events held at the Cobo Center include Autorama, the Detroit Boat Show, trade shows, conferences, and many others.

The renovations completed in 2015 guaranteed a stronger and longer commitment to keep the North American International Auto Show in downtown Detroit. New features include a three-story glass atrium

COBO CENTER

FIGURE 33. The renovated Cobo Center on the Detroit River and Detroit RiverWalk that represents one of two "green" convention centers in the United States.

linking to a new entrance that faces the Detroit River and Canada, as well as a new 40,000-square-foot ballroom with a reception capacity of 4,500 people that features floor-to-ceiling windows facing the river and open-air prefunction areas with views of downtown Detroit.

Cobo Center's primary purpose is as a generator of economic activity in southeast Michigan. As such, it now has 700,000 square feet of exhibit space, boasts one of the largest contiguous exhibit floor spaces in North America, is the seventeenth largest convention center in the country, and hosts 1.3 million visitors a year. It is also now one of only two convention centers in the United States to be LEED-certified (Leadership in Energy and Environmental Design) and designated as a "green building," complete with a 10,000-square-foot living green roof that provides habitat for birds and insects and insulation for heating and cooling the building. The green roof even includes honeybee hives and an organic herb garden (figure 34). "Bees in the D and Cobo Center are working together to make Detroit's skyline sweeter," notes Brian Peterson-Roest, Bees in the D founder. Improvements that were completed for the 2018 auto show

BEES IN THE D

FIGURE 34. Honeybee hives located on the green roof of the Cobo Center.

included a visitor observation area overlooking the green roof and new nursing pods for visiting mothers.

Ralph C. Wilson, Jr. Centennial Park

The first interim link completed by the Detroit RiverFront Conservancy on the west riverfront was West Riverfront Park , now Ralph C. Wilson, Jr. Centennial Park, located at the former *Detroit Free Press* property and behind the downtown post office. This twenty-two-acre parcel was acquired in 2007 and converted into a "green oasis" segment of the RiverWalk. Visitors now can use three new pathways linking the riverfront to West Jefferson Avenue, benches, trash receptacles, and plenty of lush green space for a variety of outdoor activities. Along this stretch, the Detroit RiverFront Conservancy expanded the width of the RiverWalk to thirty feet to provide adequate space for walking, running, biking, and fishing. Safety and security improvements include new railings, lighting, security cameras, and call boxes. Again, this is just an interim design to

FIGURE 35. Downtown Hoedown at West Riverfront Park, 2015.

provide short-term public access and simultaneously build excitement for a final, more compelling design of the park.

Centennial Park is also a new, exiting venue for waterfront concerts such as the Downtown Hoedown and Mo Pop Festival in 2015 (figure 35). Complete with the Detroit skyline and the Ambassador Bridge as backdrops, this new concert venue is an ideal setting for festival and concert action. In 2015, the Downtown Hoedown had thirty-five acts on three stages over two days and attracted approximately twenty-five thousand people over this two-day event. Attendance at the 2015 Mo Pop Festival was twelve thousand. Detroit RiverFront Conservancy is now working on connecting the Centennial Park to neighborhoods via the May Creek Greenway.

The Next Steps in the RiverWalk

In 2016, the Detroit RiverFront Conservancy initiated the development of a new strategic plan to further achieve its vision of "transforming Detroit's international riverfront, the face of the city, into a beautiful, exciting, safe, accessible, world-class gathering place for all" (Detroit RiverFront Conservancy 2018). This new strategic plan will guide the improvements to the Detroit RiverWalk over a five-year period.

As a first step, a comprehensive assessment of the state of the Detroit RiverWalk and the Detroit RiverFront Conservancy was performed. As part of the assessment, over 4,700 metropolitan Detroit residents, partners, funders, and visitors were surveyed to gain input on the future directions of the Detroit RiverFront Conservancy. Each stakeholder was asked to provide input on their current use (or nonuse) and suggestions for improvement. All were asked to provide candid feedback and to share their hopes and dreams for the RiverWalk.

These data and information were compiled and used to develop a new strategic plan that will foster a sense of ownership, enhance Detroit's image, create an inviting destination, and promote economic development. This current plan has six strategic goals:

- develop a nimble, robust, sustainable fundraising strategy (e.g., build and launch a new capital campaign; increase board involvement in fundraising)
- ensure proactive communications (e.g., new messaging for Millennials; branding; nontraditional outreach)
- ensure active leadership/board (e.g., clear roles and responsibilities for the board; self-evaluation; leadership succession plan)
- connect RiverWalk to city (e.g., Joseph Campau, Beltline, and May Creek Greenway connections to the RiverWalk; way-finding signage; water taxis and shuttles; Jefferson Avenue pedestrian crossing improvements)
- increase range of conveniences (e.g., place-making; retail, dining, and parking)
- expand educational programming (e.g., partnerships with youth-serving organizations; curricula and teachers' guides).

Concurrent with this new strategic plan, officials from the Detroit RiverFront Conservancy, the City of Detroit Planning and Development Department, and the Detroit Economic Growth Corporation developed a framework plan for Detroit's East Riverfront District. This plan coordinated efforts among the key stakeholders to preserve more riverfront land for public use and create greater community access. The plan was unveiled in 2017 and focused on what can be done in three to five years.

The boundaries of the East Riverfront District are St. Antoine to the west, East Grand Boulevard to the east, Larned Street to the north, and the Detroit River to the south. Building on the over ten-year history of the Detroit RiverFront Conservancy, the framework plan provides a functional, human-scaled vision for future developments within the East Riverfront District. It attempts to draw people together on the riverfront and hold them together. This framework plan has four strategies: parks and green open space (complete international riverfront that is inclusive and accessible); greenways (ensure safe and beautiful connections for residents to the riverfront); streetscapes (enhance mobility and safety); and development (facilitate development among local businesses and property owners while preserving the heritage of the riverfront). The plan places a high priority on action, where significant improvements will be made in a relatively short turnaround time. Examples of these actions include:

- expand Milliken State Park beginning in 2018;
- break ground on a new portion of the Detroit RiverWalk from Mt. Elliott Park to the Belle Isle Bridge (2018);
- unveil Atwater Beach project in 2018;
- begin Jefferson Avenue improvements in 2018 to provide a more pedestrian- and bicycle-friendly experience;
- start Beltline Greenway construction in 2018; and
- issue a request for proposals from the Detroit Economic Growth Corporation for adaptive reuse of the historic Stone Soap Building

MICHAEL VAN VALKENBURGH ASSOCIATES

FIGURE 36. Summer vision of the new Ralph C. Wilson, Jr. Centennial Park on the Detroit RiverWalk.

on Franklin Street for mixed-use development that will increase density along the riverfront.

Together the Detroit RiverFront Conservancy Strategic Plan and the East Riverfront District Framework Plan are good examples of getting buy-in from many stakeholder groups for complementary and reinforcing actions. It should also be noted that in 2018, the Detroit RiverFront Conservancy selected nationally acclaimed Michael Van Valkenburgh Associates to oversee final design of the Ralph C. Wilson, Jr. Centennial Park. The new vision calls for an inlet and beach as the centerpiece of this twenty-two-acre park. People will actually be able to put their toes in the

MICHAEL VAN VALKENBURGH ASSOCIATES

FIGURE 37. Winter vision of the new Ralph C. Wilson, Jr. Centennial Park on the Detroit RiverWalk.

Detroit River during summer and ice-skate in the winter (figures 36 and 37). A small island will be created offshore to restore habitat and control the flow of water to lessen erosion. There will be something for everyone at this new Centennial Park, including basketball, a beach, water slides, concert venue, fishing, places to eat, quiet reflective spots, and more.

Concluding Remarks

In a 1993 interview on National Public Radio, noted science fiction writer William Ford Gibson stated that "the future is already here—it's just not very evenly distributed" (Freud 2017). This quote helps us understand the concept of democratic design. Democratic design is a democratic approach to the design process where all stakeholders are involved and benefit. What this means is that too often society is designing a future that is less democratic and less equitable because what passes for innovative, futuristic design too often is aimed at too few. What is impressive about the Detroit RiverWalk is that it is truly designed with input from many for the benefit of all. It only takes a walk on the Detroit RiverWalk on a warm summer day to see that it is a gathering place for all. A consistent message throughout the existence of the Detroit RiverFront Conservancy is that the "riverfront belongs to all."

The first phase of the Detroit riverfront transformation, called East Riverfront, is 3.5 miles long and nearly 90 percent complete. It is estimated that nearly three million annual visitors are already using the RiverWalk amenities from Gabriel Richard Park to Joe Louis Arena. The focus of the next phase of riverfront transformation is to complete the east riverfront, connect the RiverWalk to neighborhoods through greenway trails, and provide public access along the two-mile stretch of the west riverfront from Joe Louis Arena to the Ambassador Bridge.

The Detroit RiverFront Conservancy continues to work with key stakeholders, including the city of Detroit and private property owners, toward a strategic plan for revitalizing the west riverfront. Clearly, the goal of a continuous 5.5-mile RiverWalk has not been met, but significant progress is being made. Therefore, the story is not done and more will be written.

RiverWalk stakeholders must continue to have a sense of urgency to get on with the job and must continue to ensure that there is continuous and vigorous oversight to keep the momentum going. Again, it must be remembered that the riverfront belongs to all. There is no doubt that much more needs to be done to create this public realm and sense of place, to connect to the neighborhoods and be respectful of local history and current residents, to maximize connections, and to ensure long-term sustainability. However, significant progress has been made that provides a foretaste of what is yet to come. The Detroit RiverWalk is rapidly becoming the iconographic image of Detroit in the twenty-first century. Together, the Detroit RiverWalk and a civic-mindedness that must be manifested through seven-day-a-week programming, connections and benefits to neighborhoods and other key centers of economic, entertainment, and community activities, and the successful establishment of a sense of place and stewardship can help Detroit reestablish itself as one of the great waterfront cities in the world.

CHAPTER 5

Place-Making in the D

What characteristics or amenities would make a place special or unique for you? What would it take for you to have a sense of authentic personal attachment or belonging to a particular place? What kind of a community do you want to live in? These are the kinds of questions that urban planners are grappling with today in their quest to revitalize cities and foster a more sustainable future.

Historically, urban planning and design focused primarily on buildings, but today there is a growing interest in focusing on the spaces between buildings through place-making. These spaces, rather than being seen as an afterthought, are now being viewed as an essential starting point that in turn dictates and guides other components of the community fabric. Place-making involves people in creating public spaces that will meet community needs and deliver desired community programming (Walljasper 2007). In its simplest form, place-making is the process of creating quality public places where people want to live, work, play, and learn (Silberberg et al. 2013; Bohl 2002; Schneekloth and Shibley 1995). Place-making is an inclusive process that involves local people in creating quality places for them. It involves listening to citizens about what they want for their community and working with them to assess the current state of their community, set priorities, and take action in an iterative fashion for continuous improvement of the place they want to live, work, play, and learn.

Place-making as a discipline has matured over the decades but has particularly resonated in recent years because of how its dual aim of improving the quality of a public place and improving the lives of its community has the potential to revitalize many large cities. Place-making seeks to build or improve public spaces, spark public discourse, create beauty and delight, engender civic pride, connect neighborhoods, support community health and safety, grow social justice, catalyze economic development, promote environmental sustainability, and nurture an authentic "sense of place" (Silberberg et al. 2013).

There is no doubt that Detroit has been hit hard by economic downturns, experiencing some of the highest unemployment, house foreclosure, and job loss rates in the United States. It seems almost incongruous to pursue a "sense of place" when facing such enormous economic and social challenges. But that is precisely what it is being done in Detroit, and you might be surprised to learn about place-making in the D.

This chapter will provide four examples of place-making in Detroit and will conclude with some advice for the future. Clearly, there are other examples, but these four are compelling examples of the value and benefits of place-making that can be scaled up across the entire city.

Project for Public Spaces is a nonprofit planning, design, and educational organization dedicated to helping people create and sustain public spaces that build stronger communities. It should be noted that Project for Public Spaces has been involved in Detroit place-making for nearly two decades. It has been working in and through Detroit and its citizens to catalyze place-making and help realize its many benefits.

Downtown Detroit Surrounding the Central Business District

You may have heard that Detroit's downtown is experiencing a renaissance unlike anything it has seen in decades. A key player in that renaissance is Dan Gilbert, founder and chairman of Quicken Loans Inc., the nation's second largest mortgage lender, and Rock Ventures LLC. Since 2013, Detroit-based Quicken Loans closed $200 billion in home loan volume across all fifty states, and in 2015, for the sixth consecutive year, earned J.D. Power's highest rating for client satisfaction among all U.S. mortgage lenders. Quicken Loans was ranked No. 1 on *Computerworld* magazine's "100 Best Places to Work in IT" from 2013 through 2017 and has been named one of *Fortune* magazine's "100 Best Companies to Work For" for fifteen consecutive years.

In 2013 Dan Gilbert brought together the Downtown Detroit Partnership, the Detroit Economic Growth Corporation, Project for Public Spaces, and many others to lay out a visionary place-making and retail plan for Detroit's urban core. This plan is part of the Opportunity Detroit initiative that encourages people to live, work, play, and invest in Detroit (Rock Ventures 2013).

Supporting this downtown area is the new QLINE—a 6.6-mile streetcar loop between Larned Street downtown, including the People Mover and the Detroit RiverWalk, and Grand Boulevard in the New Center Area, including its Amtrak Station that has connections to Ann Arbor, Michigan, and Chicago, Illinois, to the west, and Royal Oak and Pontiac, Michigan, to the north. It opened in 2017 and connects the city in ways it has not seen in a half century. Experience in Portland, Dallas, Denver, and Seattle has shown that such streetcar systems are a catalyst for economic growth. Approximately three thousand to five thousand people are projected to ride the QLINE daily. It will create connectivity and serve all who live, work, and play in Detroit by activating sidewalks, encouraging residents and visitors to experience all the neighborhood has to offer, from cultural institutions, restaurants, and small businesses to Detroit's entertainment district.

In the heart of downtown along Woodward Avenue is the former site of Hudson's Department Store. It opened in 1911, closed in 1983, and the structure was demolished in 1998. During its seventy-two-year history, it was the flagship store of a chain of department stores. Hudson's downtown store had more than two million square feet of retail on thirty-two floors. In 1961 it was the tallest department store in the world.

Dan Gilbert purchased this site to build an iconic building that will have ties to Detroit's past, but also represent Detroit's rebirth into a creative and high-tech future. Gilbert is building a new skyscraper (800 feet tall) that will be taller than Detroit's Renaissance Center (727 feet tall).

The design plans call for two distinct structures: an eight-hundred-foot tall residential tower with 330 residential units, and a separate structure for offices, retail, a theater, and a large public market. Between the two structures will be a sixty-foot wide, open-air promenade. There also will be a public observation deck that promises the best views of Detroit. It has been described by *Detroit Free Press* reporter John Gallagher as "a 1.5-million-square-foot mixed-use array of residential, retail, office, entertainment and civic space all wrapped up in an eye-popping architectural package" (2017). It is scheduled to open in 2020.

"The Hudson's project is a unique, once-in-a-generation opportunity that we hope will transform the landscape of downtown Detroit," said Jeff Cohen, chief executive officer of Rock Ventures (Thompson 2016). "Our vision is to create an iconic structure that all Detroiters can enjoy, while also providing additional retail, housing, and commercial space that the city needs to continue its transformation."

The redevelopment of the former Hudson's site is considered an essential building block of downtown Detroit's revival. "This is the Hudson's block development Detroiters have waited three decades to see happen," said Mayor Mike Duggan (Thompson 2016). "Its impact will be felt far beyond downtown into our neighborhoods for years to come through the construction jobs, fulltime jobs, and countless other opportunities that will be created as a result."

Dan Gilbert has invested more than $2.2 billion to purchase and renovate more than ninety commercial properties accounting for more than fourteen million square feet in the city's urban core. Thousands of jobs have been created, and today more than fifteen thousand Rock Ventures team members work in downtown Detroit. Place-making activities in this downtown area have included offering more than one thousand free events annually in four targeted parks downtown: Campus Martius, Beatrice Buck Park, Capitol Park, and Grand Circus Park. Future activities include turning Woodward into an esplanade and promenade between Jefferson to the south and Grand Circus Park to the north, and making crossing Jefferson to Hart Plaza easier and more conducive to a walkable downtown.

Probably the most outstanding example of place-making in Detroit is Campus Martius Park, located at the intersection of Woodward and Michigan Avenues, four blocks south of Grand Circus Park. In the eighteenth century it served as a military training ground (in Latin Campus Martius is loosely translated as "military ground"). After Detroit was destroyed by a fire in 1805, Judge Augustus Woodward devised a plan to remake the city in a hub-and-spoke street plan, similar to Washington, D.C. He recruited Canadian surveyors to help plot the new city's streets, parks, and lots. They set up their surveying equipment in the middle of present-day Campus Martius Park as the hub of this radial design. Eleven years later this plan was abandoned, but not before some of the most significant elements were implemented; the most prominent of these were the six primary spokes of Woodward, Michigan, Grand River, Gratiot, and Jefferson Avenues, and Fort Street.

Today, Campus Martius Park is considered by most to be the heart of the city. This 2.5-acre park anchors a two square block commercial district. It is surrounded by over 6.5 million square feet of mixed use from the stunning historic architecture of the Penobscot Building to the contemporary Compuware and Quicken Loans Headquarters, and one Kennedy Square Building.

This district is a twenty-four-hour neighborhood comprised of over twenty thousand office employees, 750 residents, over forty dining options, fifty retail outlets, the famous Westin Book Cadillac Hotel, ten thousand parking spaces, and over two million annual visitors. Place-making efforts have made Campus Martius Park into a year-round entertainment district that in 2010 was named one of the top ten public spaces in the United States by the American Planning Association. In 2010, Campus Martius was also awarded the Amanda Burden Urban Open Space Award from the Urban Land Institute, an award that celebrates and promotes vibrant, successful urban open spaces by annually recognizing and rewarding an outstanding example of a public destination that has enriched and revitalized its surrounding community. Place-making efforts are now being guided by a place-making vision for downtown Detroit called Opportunity Detroit (Rock Ventures 2013).

Partners are continuously improving place-making in Campus Martius Park as a vibrant gathering place for people to enjoy themselves during a variety of community events, such as:

- Detroit's Winter Blast that features winter activities, entertainment, and food;
- ice skating at an outdoor rink (figure 38);
- sunbathing at a beach, complete with sand, colorful seating, and umbrellas, a beach bar, and a custom deck (inspired after a similar urban beach called the Paris Plages along the Seine River);
- a bicycle sharing program;
- numerous outdoor concerts featuring live music;
- aerobic classes;
- outdoor movies for all;
- flower gardens where you can just relax;
- fountains that will delight young and old;

STEVIE ANSARA

FIGURE 38. Campus Martius Park is a year-round entertainment district that was named one of the top ten public spaces in the United States by the American Planning Association in 2010.

- art programs;
- people watching from cafes; and
- outdoor basketball courts.

Such efforts have clearly helped Campus Martius become a regional destination of choice and have helped spur major reinvestment and redevelopment efforts in surrounding blocks as part of a strategy to get more people to live, work, play, and visit downtown.

Eastern Market

Picture a beautiful summer afternoon where a saxophonist is performing his craft, barbecue smoke fills the air, people are buying their food for the week and enjoying food prepared in fashionable food trucks, and

FIGURE 39. Eastern Market is one of the oldest and largest year-round markets in the United States with over two million visitors and shoppers each year.

hundreds of conversations are going on simultaneously in one of the oldest and largest year-round markets in the United States. That is Eastern Market—a 43-acre, over 125-year-old, public market in Detroit and an outstanding example of place-making.

Eastern Market is a place that sells a variety of produce, meat, spices, baked goods, flowers, and so much more (figure 39). It also has a number of local and internationally recognized art galleries like the Red Bull House of Art, OmniCorp Detroit, and Inner State Gallery, studios, and makerspaces—community-oriented workspaces where people with common interests can meet, socialize, and collaborate.

Eastern Market is a place where people come together to enjoy healthy food and conversation, and to build a sense of community. This is evident in Eastern Market's mission of managing operations, developing programs, building facilities, providing critical infrastructure, and collaborating with community partners to strengthen the Eastern Market

District as the most inclusive, resilient, and robust regional food hub in the United States; fortify the food sector as a pillar of regional economic growth; and improve access to healthy, green, affordable, and fair food choices in Detroit and throughout southeast Michigan.

Probably the best way to describe Eastern Market is that it is like a town square—one of the few places where a wide range of people from the region regularly gather. Over two million people come to Eastern Market each year to shop and buy food. Because of this it is even sometimes called a playground for grownups.

The market has been recognized as a place of food-centered enterprise since its inception in 1891. The district is on the National Register of Historic Places and features many vendor sheds with murals and open-air markets. Surrounding the market area are many bustling food-distribution and food-processing industries. Eastern Market has played a key role in promoting entrepreneurialism across economic classes. Generations of immigrants have found their economic footing as vendors at Eastern Market. Today, Eastern Market Corporation honors that tradition with efforts to engage neighborhood-based entrepreneurs, whether they make food products or other goods. Economic democracy and community place-making define Eastern Market's authenticity. Eastern Market Corporation has adopted a ten-year plan to guide its operations. "If we do nothing, Eastern Market as we know and love it today will not be here in ten years," said Dan Carmody, president of Eastern Market Corporation (LewAllen 2016). The goals of Eastern Market's 2025 Strategy are to remain authentic, develop equity, enhance connectivity, increase density, and foster diversity (table 8). Fundamental to this is to continue to listen to a wide range of stakeholders and practice place-making via a continuous improvement process (i.e., that makes assessments, set priorities, and take actions in an iterative fashion for continuous improvement).

With its historic buildings, bustling food operations, and creative integration of art and culture, Eastern Market continues to be a vibrant place in Detroit that millions of people have an authentic personal attachment

TABLE 8. The Five Goals of Eastern Market's Ten-Year Strategy

GOAL	BRIEF DESCRIPTION	COMMENTS
Authenticity	Keep it a real, food-focused economy	The authenticity of Eastern Market rests in its over 125-year history of nourishing Detroit. As the heart of Detroit, it is a part of both the city's cultural legacy and its working economy. The future as a working food district is critical to maintaining the character of the district.
Development Equity	Enhance the market as a place of genuine economic democracy	Eastern Market must manage future development to ensure that Detroiters from traditionally underrepresented populations are key participants in the growth and development of the Eastern Market District. Economic democracy is a key feature of the market that has driven its history and made it one of Detroit's most beloved places. Beyond welcoming a wide variety of customers, Eastern Market has been the place where new immigrants and struggling households have turned to pursue their dreams that have propelled them to launch new businesses and achieve economic success. Most importantly, the opportunity to make a living in the district, for all Detroiters, must endure.
Connectivity	Bridge neighborhoods and break down barriers	The district supplies food across the entirety of the Midwest and into Canada, yet the district itself is an island, cut off by freeways and blight, despite being a ten-minute walk from Midtown or fifteen from Downtown. Strategically, Eastern Market seeks to be physically and culturally connected and accessible to all Detroiters. Overcoming the variety of barriers that divides Eastern Market from adjacent neighborhoods remains an important objective. While the completion of both the Dequindre Cut and Midtown Loop Greenways are important steps, much more work remains to better blend Eastern Market into the urban fabric. There are many opportunities ahead as Detroit rides a wave of new investment unlike anything experienced in the last sixty years.

Density	Encourage diverse growth; rebuild the urban fabric	Eastern Market, like much of Detroit, was built for more people, more work, and more activity than it has today. Eastern Market aspires to support the next generation of food businesses as well as complementary development of a lively mixed-use commercial district to greatly increase the number of jobs in the district. The increased density of food businesses and other development will provide a fundamental building block for Detroit's future.
Diversity	Increase the mix; people and food opportunities	The district is a widely recognized common ground for Detroiters, Michiganders, and visitors alike. Part of the appeal is the cross-cultural informality and the ability to find a bevy of foods at an affordable price. Diversity entails a cultural openness and variety embracing all. For this dynamic mix to continue, the range of retail, food offerings, affordability, and access must be present.

SOURCE: EASTERN MARKET CORPORATION 2016.

to. Good examples of programming that strengthens place-making at Eastern Market include:

- Market Tuesdays that features a historic market experience, plus food trucks, yoga, free Zumba, senior field trips, and youth activities;
- Saturday Market that attracts up to forty-five thousand people each week;
- the annual Flower Day, Eastern Market's signature event that attracts over 150,000 people to celebrate flowers;
- Sunday Street Market that features Detroit- and Michigan-based entrepreneurs;
- Art in the Market Tours;
- Friends of Eastern Market Cooking Days;
- Detroit Fitness events;

- a Tattoo, Art & Music Expo; and
- Eastern Market After Dark events where more than thirty venues open their doors to the public, including studios and galleries.

Wayne State University

Wayne State University is a nationally recognized metropolitan research institution, well known for its engineering and law programs and for a medical school that is one of the top in the United States. It was founded in 1868 and has evolved into a notable engine in metropolitan Detroit's educational, cultural, and economic landscape, as manifested through efforts such as its thriving research and technology park and hosting of the Detroit Windsor International Film Festival. Today, it offers more than 380 academic programs through thirteen schools and colleges to more than twenty-seven thousand students.

Wayne State University's main campus has over one hundred buildings spread across more than two hundred acres in what is known as Midtown Detroit. Midtown Detroit is a mixed-use area that has a business district, the Detroit Historical Museum, the Charles H. Wright Museum of African American History, the Detroit Institute of Arts that has been a beacon of culture for over a century, the Detroit Public Library, the College of Creative Studies, the Detroit Medical Center, several historic districts, and many art galleries, theaters, and restaurants. With such amenities it should be no surprise that Midtown Detroit has over two million annual visitors. Today, it is considered a destination of choice to live, work, and visit.

Wayne State University has become a leader in place-making. These efforts have been led out of the university's Office of Economic Development. To date over 10 percent of all students, faculty, staff, and alumni have been involved, including a team of student place-makers. The objectives of Wayne State's place-making efforts include:

- engaging a broad audience of students, faculty, staff, alumni, and community members;
- promoting transparency by sharing what activities are taking place on and around campus;
- informing future projects and activities with ongoing feedback platforms and short-term experiments;
- creating porous borders to invite the Midtown and greater Detroit community onto campus;
- having a lasting presence or physical space on campus to share place-making activities and gather ideas;
- prioritizing common interests by gathering and synthesizing the feedback it receives; and
- improving intracampus communication by facilitating the sharing of ideas across the university.

The strategy of implementing place-making initiatives is one of tactical urbanism experiments that include a suite of low-cost, temporary changes to the built urban environment that are targeted at improving campus gathering places (Lydon and Garcia 2015). Think of these efforts as quick, often temporary, inexpensive projects that can make a small part of a campus or city more lively or enjoyable. Examples of such tactical urbanism projects on campus include:

- bringing the Detroit Institute of Arts Inside-Out Program to campus (a program that places reproductions of masterpieces from the Detroit Institute of Art's collection along streets and in parks and other public places, pleasantly surprising and delighting residents);
- providing a public bicycle repair stand with an air pump;
- offering flexible public seating that invites people to interact with and enjoy unique places on campus (e.g., campus activities like the Farmers' Market, Detroit Design Festival, Student Center entrance);

FIGURE 40. Wayne State University students having fun on PARK(ing) Day, an annual, one-day event where metered parking is transformed into temporary public parks and other spaces for people to enjoy.

- expanding bicycle parking on campus;
- establishing PARK(ing) Day on campus—an annual, one-day event where artists, activists, and citizens collaborate to temporarily transform metered parking into temporary public parks and other spaces for people to enjoy (figure 40);
- improving outdoor lighting;
- adding more art to the Student Center;
- providing more live music on campus;
- expanding the Campus Farmers' Market;
- participating in the Walk Your City Campaign;
- offering outdoor games like giant chess;
- encouraging hammock use in appropriate places;

- promoting walking and bicycling for health and fitness through signage;
- ushering in the holidays each year with the popular Noel Night community event that attracts thirty thousand visitors; and
- improving way-finding signage that also helps with branding.

Future projects will include offering a food truck rally; participating in an "open streets" event that closes streets to motorized transportation and opens it to nonmotorized transportation to help encourage a sense of community; attracting more businesses and dining establishments; developing a "Pure Midtown" campaign; expanding green space on campus; and offering more live music on campus.

Wayne State University's place-making project team continues with a listening campaign consistent with the goals of place-making. The team also continues to solicit ideas and suggestions from all and to champion low-cost, temporary changes to the built urban environment in the spirit of tactical urbanism. Finally, the team is actively recruiting more partners and fund-raising through grants and crowd-sourcing.

Detroit RiverWalk

With the help of Project for Public Spaces and in partnership with Rock Ventures and other organizations, the Detroit RiverFront Conservancy has adopted a place-making philosophy of "lighter, quicker, and cheaper" developed by Reynolds (2011)—a revolutionary, low-cost, high-impact strategy for development of urban public spaces. These are simpler, easier to implement, and less expensive than projects traditionally undertaken through top-down approaches to improving cities. Indeed, Project for Public Spaces has found that expensive and labor-intensive initiatives are not the only, or even the most effective, ways to bring energy and life into a community's public space.

FIGURE 41. The popular beach volleyball court located on the Detroit RiverWalk.

Long-term improvements by the Detroit RiverFront Conservancy are clearly evidenced by the building of the 5.5-mile Detroit RiverWalk and neighborhood connections like the Dequindre Cut—a greenway trail extension heading north from the Detroit RiverWalk to Eastern Market, Midtown Detroit, and neighborhoods. United under the core principles of community vision, cost-effectiveness, collaboration, and citizen-led change, this exciting movement is championing simple, short-term, and low-cost solutions that are having remarkable impacts on the shaping of neighborhoods and cities.

The Detroit RiverFront Conservancy has created many new riverfront amenities to help transform the riverfront into the new face of the city. Examples of place-making amenities include:

- a sand beach volleyball court at Cullen Plaza (figure 41);

- comfortable chaise lounges, brightly colored Adirondack chairs and gliders, and beach sling chairs along the Detroit RiverWalk;
- oversized family-friendly lawn games like giant checkers;
- picnic tables and conversation nooks;
- mini libraries placed along the RiverWalk between Cullen Plaza and the Renaissance Center;
- a wine and beer bar for a causal drink after work;
- a new, free, outdoor fitness park called Fit Park constructed by Blue Cross and Blue Shield of Michigan and the Detroit RiverFront Conservancy on the Dequindre Cut Greenway just north of the Detroit RiverWalk (featuring six stations that promote healthy lifestyles); and
- a birding station on the Detroit RiverWalk at Gabriel Richard Park overlooking the Detroit River and Belle Isle, featuring four bird-spotting scopes and an interpretive panel that identifies common birds that can be seen.

Such place-making amenities are being complemented with programming of the Detroit RiverWalk to help make Detroit a fun place to live, work, and play. For example, Rivière28, the conservancy's active professionals auxiliary, organizes several fun, funky events each summer along the RiverWalk, including Light Up the Riverfront and Soiree on the Greenway, designed to attract hundreds of young professionals to meet and have fun on the riverfront. These events typically feature live music, food, and an urban campfire with the Detroit River as a backdrop. Other popular programming events include:

- a senior walking program called RiverWalkers that attracts up to 1,400 walkers each Tuesday and Thursday (sponsored by Detroit Medical Center);
- Walk the RiverWalk Wednesdays sponsored by Blue Cross Blue Shield;

- weekly herbal walk and talk program;
- free yoga and t'ai chi classes on the RiverWalk, and Body Love Fit Camp on the Dequindre Cut;
- an annual Riverfront Run;
- weekly Canine to Five group dog walks on the RiverWalk;
- weekly ComePlay sand volleyball league;
- weekly Detroit Experience Factory riverfront tours;
- an annual Touch-A-Truck event that allows children to get hands-on experiences with many types of large trucks, like front-end loaders, dump trucks, excavators, emergency vehicles, tractors, and snow plows;
- the annual GM River Days that features musical acts, a Kids Zone, outdoor recreational activities organized by the Michigan Department of Natural Resources, a carnival midway, a Taste of Detroit food court, boat tours, Jet Ski performances, and more;
- Reading and Rhythm on the Riverfront—a literacy-based family-friendly program for nearly four thousand children made possible by the General Motors Foundation;
- General Motors' Rockin' on the Riverfront Concerts;
- outdoor concerts at Chene Park;
- jazz performances at Roberts Riverwalk Hotel;
- a Mo Pop Festival at Ralph C. Wilson, Jr. Centennial Park featuring a wide variety of popular music concerts;
- movie nights on the riverfront;
- a Riverfront Mexican Festival;
- a Green Day that features rain barrel–making workshops;
- quarterly birding events organized by the Detroit Audubon Society and the U.S. Fish and Wildlife Service for kids and families;
- an annual Kids Fishing Fest that attracts four hundred children, many to have their first fishing experience; and
- an annual sturgeon day that provides an interactive educational

experience to school children on the life history and population status of one of the Great Lakes' most mysterious and interesting inhabitants.

A total of thirty-two partners helped deliver these programming events along the Detroit RiverWalk during 2016, attracting 301,170 people.

Detroit Future City

The work of Detroit Future City must also be acknowledged in citywide place-making. Detroit Future City (2012) is a comprehensive, innovative plan for reshaping the city of Detroit over the next fifty years. The planning team engaged Detroiters through hundreds of meetings, thirty thousand conversations, over seventy thousand surveys, and countless hours of working meetings to critically analyze data about the city. The final plan breaks down necessary actions into several key focus areas: neighborhoods, city systems, land use, public lands, and civic engagement.

Once the plan was complete, a Detroit Future City Implementation Office was established to translate the guiding principles of the Detroit Future City Strategic Framework into practice. This implementation office is an independent, nonprofit organization governed by an independent board of directors. The Detroit Future City plan is now becoming the framework under which a citywide place-making effort is being implemented through the Detroit Future City Implementation Office. In 2017, the office released a five-year strategic plan that calls for using open space as part of land-use policy, supporting ecosystems to reduce stormwater overflows, and improving existing single-family rental properties. In particular, this strategic plan will laser focus on improvements in Detroit's neighborhoods.

Concluding Remarks

Most people recognize that Detroit's riverfront was the birthplace of the fur trade, shipbuilding, and industry. By the late 1900s Detroit's working riverfront, which supported much industry and commerce, had gone through considerable decline, with fewer people and industries and much underutilized and undervalued riverfront land. Today, the Detroit RiverFront Conservancy has been reimaging the riverfront as a multiuse gathering place for all in a fashion that can redefine the city. However, this cannot be done in isolation. Place-making along the Detroit River-Walk must become part of a larger network of community places like Midtown, the Wayne State University campus, Eastern Market, and the neighborhoods.

Research has shown that there are probably as many place-making methods as there are place-making stakeholders. Place-making efforts need a zealous champion—one who is a single-minded, tireless, passionate advocate and a great connector that meaningfully engages and involves the community (Silberberg et al. 2013). More place-making champions need to be developed in and for Detroit.

Experience has shown that the collaborations and iterative, continuous-improvement actions inherent in place-making nourish communities and empower people (Silberberg et al. 2013). Project for Public Spaces identified four key attributes to successful place-making: accessible; active; comfortable; and sociable (table 9). These attributes must be lived up to in future planning initiatives. There must also be a long-term commitment to place-making for continuous improvement, consistent with adaptive management where assessments are made, priorities set, and actions taken in an iterative fashion for continuous improvement. If the above attributes can be lived up to and a long-term commitment to place-making can be made and followed up on, then Detroit has a better chance of redefining itself as a comeback city and model of sustainable redevelopment.

TABLE 9. Four Key Attributes to Successful Place-Making as Defined by Project for Public Spaces

ATTRIBUTE	DESCRIPTION
Accessibility	• Walkable • Convenient • Easy to access and get through • Visible from a distance and up close • High parking turnover • Convenient to public transit
Active	• Fun • Engaging • Activities that give people a reason to return
Comfortable	• Attractive • Clean • Safe • Providing places to sit
Sociable	• Neighborly • Welcoming • Meeting and greeting neighbors • Feeling comfortable interacting with strangers

SOURCE: ROCK VENTURES 2013.

CHAPTER 6

Greenways, Blueways, and Flyways

D
uring the Industrial Revolution most North American cities made rivers their back door. Today, most cities pursuing sustainability and its concomitant competitive advantage are working to make rivers their front door and to ensure that rivers run through the life of their communities. Indeed, Chappell (2007) concluded that in merging nature and culture the most successful cities combine such universal needs as maintaining or restoring contact with the cycles of nature with specific, local characteristics.

The Detroit RiverWalk is reconnecting people to the Detroit River and helping make outdoor and nature experiences part of everyday urban life. It was indeed quite prophetic that the great American author and naturalist Henry David Thoreau, while watching civilization expand into the countryside during his lifetime (1817–62), recommended that every town should have a forest of five hundred to one thousand acres to be used for conservation instruction and outdoor recreation (Malnor and Malnor 2009). John Muir in his seminal book *The Yosemite* (1912, 256) poetically described the importance of nature experiences in everyday life as follows: "Everyone needs beauty as well as bread, places to play in and pray in, where nature may heal and cheer and give strength to the body and soul."

The Detroit RiverFront Conservancy is building the Detroit RiverWalk as a gathering place for all to enjoy and benefit from. It should also be noted that reconnecting people to the land and water through compelling outdoor recreational and educational experiences helps foster an appreciation and love for the outdoors. That, in turn, helps develop a strong sense of place that inspires positive actions, a sense of ownership, and stewardship for the community's natural capital.

One of the challenges for the Detroit RiverFront Conservancy is to become more relevant to its citizens who have many competing priorities and few outdoor experiences. There is no doubt that we need to find ways and means to connect with young people who are technologically fluent but deficient in outdoor/nature experiences. This chapter will provide three compelling examples of how people are being reconnected to the Detroit River through engagement in compelling outdoor recreational and educational experiences and will conclude with thoughts on where the Detroit RiverFront Conservancy needs to go in the future.

Greenways

Greenways are a way to get people outdoors and have fun. They have also been described as tangible gifts to the future that encourage us to walk, hike, and bike. Greenway trails are hard-surfaced paths that most often have minimal grade and provide free public access for nonmotorized uses like bicycling, walking, running, skating, and wheelchair access. Greenways often link parks, nature areas, cultural features, or historic sites with each other, for recreational and conservation purposes. They are sometimes called linear parks because they preserve ribbons of nature that often follow stream corridors and abandoned railroad right-of-ways.

Based on experience throughout North America, greenways promote outdoor recreation, catalyze economic development, increase adjacent property values, celebrate historical and cultural assets, promote conservation and environmental education, support healthful living, and improve quality of life. Greenways can also provide an exceptional outdoor recreational experience that reconnects children and families to natural resources that, in turn, can help build a stewardship ethic. It should not be surprising that greenways are an enormous source of community pride.

Detroit and Windsor, Ontario, share the same ecosystem and have much in common culturally, socially, economically, and historically. Each has a unique greenway system. In many respects, southwest Ontario's greenway trails have been an inspiration to the development of southeast Michigan's greenway trails. The city of Windsor maintains 79.5 miles of trails, including the Windsor Loop, a 26.4-mile loop that when completed, will traverse around the city's perimeter, joining neighborhoods and providing access to the Trans Canada Trail. The longest greenway trail in Windsor's network is the Roy A. Battagello River Walk (built in the late 1960s and upgraded/widened several times), stretching from west of the Ambassador Bridge to the historical Hiram Walker Distillery, a distance of about five miles.

The new Rt. Hon. Herb Gray Parkway trails offer an additional 12.4 miles of greenways. As well, the Waterfront Regeneration Trust added Lake Erie to the Waterfront Trail, signing 375 miles of new trail from Fort Erie (near Niagara Falls) to Windsor and Lakeshore on Lake St. Clair. The new route connects twenty-seven new waterfront communities.

In Essex County, the thirty-one-mile Chrysler Canada Greenway is a multiuse rail trail that is the southernmost section of the Trans Canada Trail. Managed by Essex Region Conservation Authority, it connects a number of communities and natural areas in Essex County and the heart of southwest Ontario's wine country. Along the Chrysler Canada Greenway cyclists can see unique natural resources, rich agricultural lands, historically and architecturally significant structures, and award-winning wineries. The new Cypher Systems Group Greenway is a 13.7-mile rail trail that connects Essex to Amherstburg.

In southeast Michigan, greenways have been championed by the Community Foundation for Southeast Michigan, Detroit Greenways Coalition, the Downriver Linked Greenways Initiative, the Greater Detroit American Heritage River Initiative, the Michigan Rails-to-Trails Conservancy, and numerous communities. Although considerable planning was done for nearly three decades, greenway construction and development did not occur substantially until the late 1990s. Considerable progress has been made in the last ten to fifteen years:

- The Community Foundation for Southeast Michigan invested $25 million in greenways, which leveraged an addition $90 million to construct over one hundred miles of greenways in southeast Michigan.
- The Downriver Linked Greenways Initiative has championed the construction of over fifty miles of continuous greenways in the watershed of the lower Detroit River.
- The Detroit RiverFront Conservancy has raised over $163 million in twelve years to construct the Detroit RiverWalk in downtown Detroit, representing one of the largest urban waterfront development projects, by scale, in the United States.
- Detroit Greenways Coalition has championed building greenways throughout the city of Detroit for all, including a twenty-six-mile inner circle greenway named the Joe Louis Greenway.

Detroit's land area is massive—139 square miles. You can fit all of Boston, San Francisco, and the borough of Manhattan inside the footprint of Detroit. This large land mass is clearly a challenge when it comes to

DETROIT GREENWAYS COALITION

FIGURE 42. Bicycling on the Detroit RiverWalk that won a prestigious Excellence in the Waterfront Award from the Waterfront Center.

greenways. Detroit Greenways Coalition is the primary organization working—segment by segment and link by link—to create a citywide greenway network. Thus far, Detroit has over two hundred miles of bike routes and greenways. The Detroit RiverWalk, which won an Excellence in the Waterfront Award from the Waterfront Center, connects inland via the Dequindre Cut Greenway (figure 42). The Dequindre Cut Greenway is a former Grand Trunk Railroad line that is below street level and runs from Atwater Street at the Detroit RiverWalk to Mack Avenue and Eastern Market. In May 2016 alone, over fifteen thousand bicyclists and over five thousand walkers used the cut. The Dequindre Cut is part of a network of routes for cyclists and pedestrians between the Detroit RiverWalk, Eastern Market, Midtown, the New Center Area, Hamtramck, and neighborhoods in between. It will soon link to the Joe Louis Greenway that encircles the city of Detroit and connects to the cities of Hamtramck, Highland Park, and Dearborn.

Detroit's greenways are connected to over eight hundred miles of greenway trails in southeast Michigan. Of particular interest is the Iron Belle Trail that when complete, will link the wealth of natural and cultural resources in the state, including a hiking and biking route connecting Belle Isle in Detroit to Ironwood in Michigan's Upper Peninsula. The route heads south from Belle Isle via the Southwest Detroit Greenlink and through ten downriver communities, primarily following the emerging route of the Downriver Linked Greenways Initiative. The biking route heads north from Belle Isle via the Conner Creek Greenway.

Both southwest Ontario's and southeast Michigan's greenway systems are unique individually, but together they are truly world-class. In 2016, U.S. and Canadian greenway partners joined forces to develop a Canada–U.S. Greenways Vision Map to encourage people to grab their bikes and explore both sides of the Detroit River (figure 43). The group released a binational greenways vision map to connect emerging international greenways, trails, and bike lanes, establishing safe and convenient routes for pedestrians and bicyclists. Partners in this project included Bike Friendly Windsor Essex, the Canadian Consulate General, the city of Detroit, the city of Windsor, Community Foundation for Southeast Michigan, Detroit Greenways Coalition, Detroit Metro Convention & Visitors Bureau, Detroit RiverFront Conservancy, Detroit/Wayne County Port Authority, Downtown Detroit Partnership, Essex County, Essex Region Conservation Authority, National Park Service, Tourism Windsor Essex Pelee Island, U.S. Fish and Wildlife Service, Wheelhouse Detroit, and Windsor Bicycling Committee.

It is the vision of these Canadian and U.S. partners to encourage stronger linkages between emerging greenways of southwest Ontario and southeast Michigan via a future dedicated bike lane on the new Gordie Howe Bridge and a possible future ferry system between Windsor and Detroit. This vision map encourages people to grab their bicycle and explore both sides of the Detroit River, the only river system in North America to receive both Canadian and American Heritage River

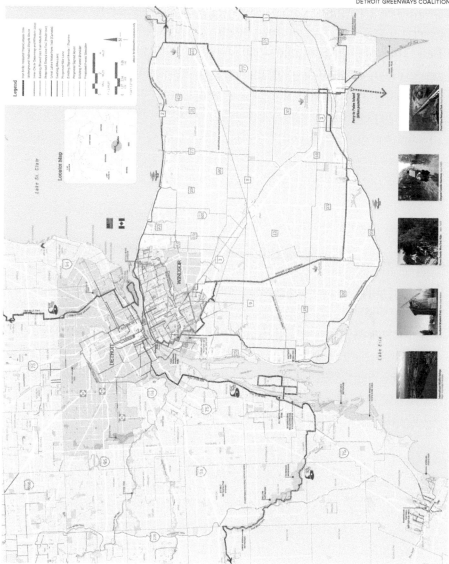

FIGURE 43. U.S.–Canada Greenways Vision Map.

Initiative designations, as well as the only international wildlife refuge in North America (i.e., Detroit River International Wildlife Refuge). Todd Scott, executive director of the Detroit Greenways Coalition, notes that "significant investments have been made that improve biking and walking opportunities on both sides of the river. This map highlights the need to build cross-border connections for those traveling on foot or by bike" (press release, 24 April 2016) Jennifer Leitzinger, transportation planning engineer with the city of Windsor, notes that "this map clearly identifies the locations of the cycling facilities on both sides of the border, which in turn encourages international adventures" (press release, 24 April 2016).

In 2017, the Windsor–Detroit Bridge Authority announced, following considerable advocacy, that the new Gordie Howe Bridge will include a dedicated multiuse path that will accommodate pedestrians and cyclists. The integration of safe, separated bike and pedestrian lanes on the new Gordie Howe Bridge will be a clear benefit to communities on both sides of the border, as it will support active transportation, a healthy lifestyle, and bicycle tourism in southwest Ontario and southeast Michigan. This new bridge is scheduled to open in 2024.

Blueways

Rivers, lakes, and streams are among America's most treasured natural resources. There has been growing interest in establishing a river version of a greenway trail ("blueway" or water trail) that provides opportunities for canoeing, kayaking, and small boat paddling. These blueways typically have a number of launch points where paddlers can get up close and enjoy water resources. Benefits of these blueways include getting people into the outdoors, creating a sense of place, raising environmental awareness, promoting a stewardship ethic, promoting good health through outdoor recreation, and boosting ecotourism.

The Outdoor Foundation has shown that participation in these paddle sports is increasing. For example, 21.7 million Americans or 7.4 percent of the population enjoyed paddling in 2014. This represents an increase of more than three million participants since the study began in 2010. Paddlers averaged seven annual outings in 2014, up from 6.8 the previous year. In total, there were 216 million paddling outings in 2014 (The Outdoor Foundation 2015).

This study also found that kayaking is the most popular form of paddling, increasing from 3 percent of Americans participating in 2010 to 4.4 percent in 2014. Kayakers are also the most avid paddlers, averaging 8.1 outings a year. Kayaking is most popular among young adults, ages eighteen to twenty-four. Interestingly, a majority of kayakers in this age group (62 percent) are female (The Outdoor Foundation 2015).

To address this interest and meet this demand, Metropolitan Affairs Coalition, a nonprofit organization made up of business, government, labor, and educational leaders dedicated to building consensus and seeking solutions to regional issues in metropolitan Detroit, developed a vision plan for a Detroit Heritage River Water Trail in 2006. Metropolitan Affairs Coalition brought together, under its Greater Detroit American Heritage River Initiative, numerous partners, including the Downriver Linked Greenways Initiative, Friends of the Detroit River, Huron-Clinton Metropolitan Authority, Michigan Sea Grant, National Park Service, the U.S. Fish and Wildlife Service, and Wayne County Parks. These partners then developed a vision plan for this blueway that would both promote existing, close-to-home, paddle-based recreational opportunities and plan for future expansion of ecotourism.

In 2013, the vision plan was updated to a usable water trail map that identifies both paddling access points and paddling routes (figure 44). The Detroit Heritage River Water Trail extends some thirty-eight miles from Maheras-Gentry Park at the upper end of the Detroit River to Luna Pier on western Lake Erie in the southern end of Monroe County. Kayakers can paddle through time along waterways that sustained Native

FIGURE 44. Detroit Heritage River Water Trail along the Detroit River and western Lake Erie.

Americans, supported the fur trade, fostered the Industrial Revolution, and are now heralded as North America's only international wildlife refuge. Along the way, paddlers can see the 980-acre island park designed by Frederick Law Olmstead (Belle Isle), the oldest rowing club (Detroit Rowing Club) in the United States established in 1839, the international crossing of the Underground Railroad where forty thousand freedom seekers gained their freedom, the historical dry-dock area where 650 freighters were built during the shipbuilding era, the industries that made Detroit the "arsenal of democracy," and truly exceptional wildlife, including waterfowl, egrets, bald eagles, herons, and countless fish being landed by anglers. Such paddling experiences are reconnecting people to the rich biodiversity and exceptional natural resources in their backyard.

RIVERSIDE KAYAK CONNECTION

FIGURE 45. Kayaking in the Detroit River along the Detroit RiverWalk.

A user guide is also available for outdoor enthusiasts to plan paddling trips along the Detroit Heritage River Water Trail (a printed version is available from Riverside Kayak Connection; info@riversidekayak.com). This guide offers detailed descriptions of each location, a key feature in designing your outdoor adventure. It also details the newest launch sites, updated information on existing locations, safety suggestions, and resources for local paddling groups. Recommended paddling routes are also highlighted, presenting not only mileage but water time and possible conditions.

Paddling access to waters adjacent to the Detroit RiverWalk is currently provided at Belle Isle, Maheras-Gentry Park, and launches at the end of Alter Road. Paddlers can launch at either of these locations and enjoy the Detroit RiverWalk from a water perspective (figure 45).

Alex Howbert grew up kayaking on the canals on the east end of the

Detroit River and racing sailboats on the Detroit River and Lake St. Clair. His passion for watersports on the Detroit River led him to buy an old marina and start a business that would help make the river and canals more accessible to people. "We have a beautiful resource right here, and it's difficult for people to access unless they have a boat," notes Howbert, founder of Detroit River Sports (Wos 2017, 1). For six years he and his staff have been giving tours that paddle through the canals surrounding Grayhaven Island and by the old Fisher Mansion, around Belle Isle and Peche Isle, along the RiverWalk and past the Renaissance Center, and even as far down as historic Fort Wayne. "Even tough people have lived here their entire lives, they don't even know the canals exist," notes manager and tour guide Julie MacDonald (Wos 2017, 2). Detroit River Sports even hosts a Paddle to the Table event where, after paddling the river, they partner with Coriander Kitchen and Farm to offer a memorable outdoor dinner on the marina dock. All of this is targeted at reconnecting people with the amazing Detroit River right in our backyard. MacDonald notes "Being out on open water, you forget you are in the middle of a huge metropolitan city" (Wos 2017, 3).

Riverside Kayak Connection, a metropolitan Detroit kayak outfitter, offers a variety of services and free events to promote paddle sports from Belle Isle and Milliken State Park's Outdoor Adventure Center on the Detroit RiverWalk. On Belle Isle, Riverside Kayak Connection also operates a kayak livery in the historic Flynn Pavilion that is located on the canals, offers classes, and hosts a demonstration day where people can try out different types of kayaks.

For the future there is interest in creating paddle-up access to Marshall's Bar, a historically infamous speakeasy with a basement door previously used by bootlegger boats and offering excursions out of Chene Park Amphitheater on the banks of the Detroit River, where floating boaters could see concerts from the water. Clearly, when most people think about kayaking and canoeing, they think about paddling through pristine rivers or lakes, or through streams running through wilderness areas or forests. However, paddling enthusiasts along the Detroit River are saying think again. Detroit River paddlers can get an unparalleled experience of paddling along the Detroit RiverWalk, through the industrial heartland, among freighters and skyscrapers, and through North America's only international wildlife refuge, the Detroit River International Wildlife Refuge. Michigan residents agree. In 2015 Michigan residents, through a Michigan Department of Natural Resources survey, identified the Detroit Heritage River Water Trail as one of the "Top 11" Water Trails in Michigan.

Flyways

Why should we care about birds? Melanie Driscoll, director of bird conservation for the Gulf of Mexico and the Mississippi Flyway at the National Audubon Society notes:

> Birds are important because they keep systems in balance: they pollinate plants, disperse seeds, scavenge carcasses, and recycle nutrients back into the earth. But they also feed our spirits, marking for us the passage of the seasons, moving us to create art and poetry, inspiring us to flight, and reminding us that we are not only on, but of, this earth. (The Editors 2013, 1)

You might be surprised at just how many people go bird watching. According to the U.S. Fish and Wildlife Service (Carver 2013) there are about forty-seven million Americans over the age of sixteen who go bird watching each year. The U.S. Fish and Wildlife Service has estimated that trip-related and equipment-related expenditures associated with bird watching generated nearly $107 billion in total industry output, 666,000 jobs, and $13 billion in local, state, and federal tax revenue (Carver 2013).

You might also be surprised to know that there are unique birding opportunities in metropolitan Detroit and along the Detroit River. The Detroit River is at the intersection of two major North American flyways—the Atlantic and Mississippi. Over three hundred thousand diving ducks, seventy-five thousand shorebirds, and hundreds of thousands of land birds and fall raptors frequent the shoreline habitats to rest, nest, and feed (Hartig, Robinson, and Zarull 2010). Over 30 species of waterfowl, 23 species of raptors, 31 species of shorebirds, and 160 species of songbirds are found along or migrate through this corridor (Hartig, Robinson, and Zarull 2010). This avian biodiversity and the diversity of habitats to support these birds have given the region international acclaim. The Detroit River and western Lake Erie have been recognized for their biodiversity in the North American Waterfowl Management Plan, the United Nations Convention on Biological Diversity, the Western Hemispheric Shorebird Reserve Network, the Biodiversity Investment Area Program of Environment Canada and U.S. Environmental Protection Agency, and in recent years as North America's only international wildlife refuge (Hartig, Robinson, and Zarull 2010).

Birds can make the Detroit RiverWalk a chance for discovery. For a young child or a seasoned birder, birds can inspire a sense of wonder and remind us that nature is not just up north, but truly in the D. For a bird watcher every walk is filled with anticipation. What feathered friend might I see next?

Without a doubt the best place to watch birds along the Detroit RiverWalk is at the far eastern end at the 980-acre Belle Isle State Park. Belle Isle is a great place to see migrant and wintering waterfowl. It is also a well-kept secret during the songbird migration in spring and fall, when the swamp woods on the eastern end can be filled with warblers, thrushes, and sparrows. Allen Chartier, a long-term birding expert from Detroit, has recorded many times over twenty species of warbler in the spring, including golden-winged, hooded, and prothonotary warblers. He recently observed on Belle Isle the first pileated woodpecker in Wayne

County in more than one hundred years. The birding experience is also excellent in other seasons as evidenced by the following quote from Allen Chartier:

> One fall day in 2005 I experienced hundreds each of white-throated sparrow, yellow-rumped warbler, both kinglets, and hermit and Swainson's thrushes, many feeding on the abundant food crop in the swamp woods. Northern saw-whet owls also migrate through Belle Isle, and sometimes overwinter in the tangles in the woods. (2007, 1)

Detroit Audubon Society has recorded over 350 species of birds in the Detroit River corridor. With knowledge of this avian biodiversity and the many exceptional birding opportunities in the Detroit-Windsor metropolitan area, Metropolitan Affairs Coalition, the U.S. Fish and Wildlife Service, Michigan Sea Grant, the International Wildlife Refuge Alliance, Wild Birds Unlimited, and the National Fish and Wildlife Foundation developed a unique "Byways to Flyways" bird driving tour map to promote twenty-seven exceptional birding sites throughout the Windsor-Detroit metropolitan area (figure 46). Included within these sites are many Important Bird Areas identified by the National Audubon Society, two "Wetlands of International Importance" identified under the international Ramsar Convention (i.e., Point Pelee National Park in Ontario and Humbug Marsh in Michigan), several Christmas Bird Count sites, and two internationally recognized hawk watch sites. These world-class birding opportunities are helping to reconnect Detroiters to nature right in their backyard and to enjoy an outdoor pastime that over forty-seven million people in the United States enjoy.

Recognizing the importance of this region in bird migration and conservation, the U.S. Fish and Wildlife Service designated metropolitan Detroit as the twenty-ninth Urban Bird Treaty city in the United States. The Urban Bird Treaty program is a collaborative effort among federal, state, and municipal agencies, nongovernmental organizations, and

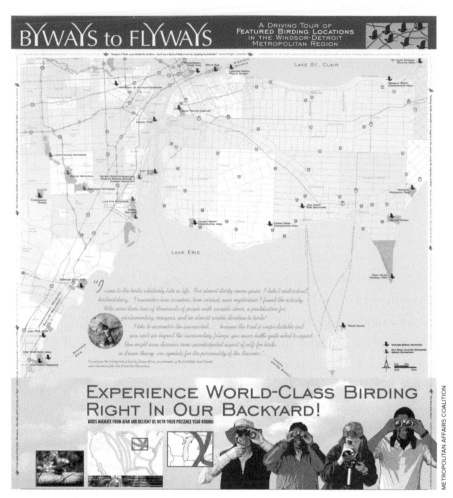

FIGURE 46. Byways to Flyways bird driving tour map.

academic institutions to create bird-friendly environments and provide citizens, especially youth, with opportunities to connect with nature through birding and conservation (Metro Detroit Nature Network 2017). The program emphasizes habitat conservation through invasive species control, native plant restoration, bird-safe building programs, bird and habitat monitoring, and education programs.

Concluding Remarks

The Detroit RiverWalk has become an urban getaway for outdoor recreation. Because of close-to-home greenways, blueways, and flyways
Detroit residents don't have to drive four or more hours to get an exceptional outdoor recreational experience. Interest in greenways, blueways,
and flyways is increasing. However, a sizeable urban population remains
disconnected from the outdoors and natural resources.

The U.S. Fish and Wildlife Service (2011) has recognized the urgent
need to connect an ever-growing and disconnected urban population
to the outdoors and its natural resources. To address this need, the U.S.
Fish and Wildlife Service has established an Urban Wildlife Conservation
Program. This program has undertaken a critical analysis of conservation relevance in urban areas and of how to create a connected urban
conservation constituency. Out of this critical analysis, the U.S. Fish and
Wildlife Service (2013) identified that excellence in urban wildlife refuges
is achieved when the following standards are met:

- connect urban people with nature using a full spectrum of
  opportunities for "nature novices" through in-depth adventurous
  programs
- build partnerships
- become a community asset
- ensure adequate long-term resources
- provide equitable access
- ensure that visitors feel safe and welcome
- showcase sustainability in all actions and activities.

Such standards are also relevant to the work of the Detroit RiverFront
Conservancy and its mission of "transforming Detroit's international
riverfront—the face of the city—into a beautiful, exciting, safe, and

accessible world-class gathering place for all" (Detroit RiverFront Conservancy 2018). A high priority must be placed on completing Detroit's twenty-six-mile Joe Louis Greenway and completing connections to the Detroit RiverWalk and neighborhoods, expanding the Detroit Heritage River Water Trail and paddling opportunities for all, and expanding birding and other outdoor conservation experiences for all to help reestablish connection to the Detroit River. This, in turn, can help create a sense of place and help lead to the development of a stewardship ethic.

CHAPTER 7

Economic Benefits

M ore than 140 million Americans make outdoor recreation a priority in their daily lives—and they prove it with their wallets. Each year, Americans spend $646 billion on outdoor recreation (Outdoor Industry Association 2012). That is why it is no longer something nice for communities to have, but a vital cornerstone of all successful communities that see the undeniable economic, social, and health benefits of outdoor recreation.

Metropolitan Detroit is blessed with abundant and diverse natural resources, including rivers, lakes, natural areas, world-class fisheries, and continentally significant wildlife. These natural resources support outdoor recreation for residents, enhance quality of life, attract visitors, help sustain our manufacturing and energy sectors, and help attract and retain employees for all businesses.

Recently, Business Leaders for Michigan, Public Sector Accountants, and Sustainable Water Works (2015) developed a business plan for natural resources to support a healthy and sustainable economy in Michigan.

This Michigan Natural Resources Business Plan identifies five strategies to promote a healthy economy and help achieve competitive advantage:

- improve public infrastructure that supports Michigan's natural resources industries, particularly rail and highway improvements that support export of agriculture, timber, and mining products, and improve the efficiency and access to highly demanded tourism destinations in Michigan
- expand and enhance tourism and outdoor recreation amenities and services, and continue to expand the national and international promotion of Michigan's tourism assets, in order to increase the number of visitors to the state and tourism-serving businesses/jobs in Michigan
- focus the state's existing public and private research and development assets on making Michigan a national leader in the innovation of sustainable natural resources products and processes
- provide an attractive and affordable working environment in order to ensure an adequate labor force to support the growth of Michigan's natural resources industries
- ensure dedicated leadership and accountability for the implementation of this natural resources business plan.

Two of these strategies (expand and enhance tourism and outdoor recreation, and provide an attractive and affordable working environment) pertain to the Detroit RiverFront Conservancy's mission of "transforming Detroit's international riverfront—the face of the city—into a beautiful, exciting, safe, and accessible world-class gathering place for all" (Detroit RiverFront Conservancy 2018).

This chapter will provide examples of how the investments in the Detroit RiverWalk and investments in expanding close-to-home outdoor recreation in the metropolitan Detroit area are reaping substantial economic benefits that enhance our economy. Indeed, the efforts of the

Detroit RiverFront Conservancy and its partners are realizing surprising return on investments.

Economic Benefits of the Detroit RiverWalk

Ten years into the Detroit RiverFront Conservancy's work to build the Detroit RiverWalk, the conservancy took stock of where they came from, how far they had come, and what was the economic return on investment as of 2012. The Detroit RiverFront Conservancy hired CSL International (2013) to undertake an economic impact study of the Detroit RiverWalk at the conclusion of its first ten years.

This economic benefits study of reclaiming Detroit's downtown, industrial waterfront as public greenspace reported that as of 2012 the east riverfront portion of the Detroit RiverWalk that stretches over 3.5 miles was 80 percent complete, with the remaining 20 percent in planning or under construction. CSL International (2013) found that nearly three million annual visitors were using the Detroit RiverWalk and its associated green infrastructure. As of 2012, over one hundred events were held along the riverfront, ranging from small weekly gatherings to large annual events like River Days Festival.

The 3.5 miles of the Detroit RiverWalk completed as of 2012 were constructed at a cost of $80 million. In addition, a $60 million endowment was created for long-term operation and maintenance (CSL International 2013). This investment was a catalyst for $1.55 billion in total public- and private-sector investment (including the value of contributed land), of which approximately $639 million can be directly linked to riverfront improvements (table 10). In addition, there is potential for an additional $700–950 million investment in the future (CSL International 2013).

CSL International (2013) concluded its economic impact study stating that the 3.5 miles of Detroit RiverWalk completed as of 2012 had spurred approximately $1 billion in total public- and private-sector

TABLE 10. Summary of Detroit RiverWalk Economic Impacts in the First Ten Years

CONSTRUCTION IMPACTS	
Riverfront Construction and Land Value	$1.548 billion
Portion Attributable to Riverfront	$639 million
Construction Period Jobs	16,700
ANNUAL IMPACTS	
Total Annual Spending	$43.7 million
Combined Annual Spending, 2003–2013	$360.6 million
Annual Positive Media Value	$600,000
Annual Jobs	1,300
Total Annual Tax Revenue Generation	$4.5 million

SOURCE: CSL INTERNATIONAL 2013.

LEO WEISSBURG

FIGURE 47. Orleans Landing, that has been built along the Detroit RiverWalk and adjacent to the Outdoor Adventure Center, is a good example of catalyzing economic development.

investment (figure 47). Further, given the improvements to the economy and financial markets nationally, the investment totals tied to the Detroit RiverWalk over the next ten years is projected to exceed another $1 billion. Total annual spending by visitors, residents, employees, and other operations along the Detroit RiverWalk was estimated to be $43.7 million. As of 2012, building the 3.5 miles of the Detroit RiverWalk had supported 16,700 construction jobs during the ten-year construction period and provided 1,300 ongoing, annual jobs. Of the three million annual visitors, 90 percent of their visits would not have taken place without the significant riverfront improvements. Clearly, these data show a substantial return on investment in building the Detroit RiverWalk with more economic benefits yet to come. Such economic rationale should also help attract future funding partners to complete the Detroit RiverWalk and to fully fund the endowment to operate, maintain with quality, program, and steward this public space in perpetuity.

Economic Benefits of Greenways

Numerous studies show that greenway trails and green space are important community assets that can help spur economic development. From urban home buyers preferring to live along or near a greenway trail to bicyclists and hikers making their way through the city or to a nature area, park, or cultural center, greenways attract people and dollars (figure 48). The Urban Land Institute (2016) has identified four ways that greenways boost economic growth: increasing retail visibility and sales volume, fueling redevelopment to boost real estate value, helping communities attract and retain talented workers, and making workers healthier and more productive.

The San Antonio River Walk is a key part of the cultural fabric of San Antonio, Texas, contributing greatly to the quality of life of local residents. It is one of Texas's leading tourist attractions and is also an

DETROIT GREENWAYS COALITION

FIGURE 48. The Detroit RiverWalk is a community asset that attracts people and spurs economic development.

important driver of the local economy. An economic impact study performed by Nivin (2014) showed that there were 11.5 million visitors to the River Walk during the twelve-month period of study: 9.3 million nonresident visitors whose main reason for coming to the area was to visit the River Walk and approximately 2.2 million trips made to the River Walk by residents. Nivin (2014) found that these residents and visitors spend about $2.4 billion each year, which supports more than thirty-one thousand jobs. The people in these jobs earn incomes and benefits of over $1 billion. The economic impact is about $3.1 billion per year. This economic activity resulted in approximately $173 million flowing to state and local governments and almost $201 million in revenues being generated for the federal government (Nivin 2014).

The Virginia Creeper Trail is a thirty-four-mile long rail trail with trailheads in Abington and Whitetop Station, Virginia. Bowker et al.

(2004) performed a study to estimate annual trail usage, examine user attitudes/preferences, and estimate economic impacts and benefits. Virginia Creeper Trail users, including local residents and visitors, spent about $2.5 million over a twelve-month period spanning 2002–3 related to their recreational visits. Of this amount, nonlocal visitor spending was about $1.2 million in Washington and Grayson counties. This nonlocal visitor spending in the area generated $1.6 million in economic impacts and supported close to thirty jobs.

The Urban Land Institute (2015) has reported that 50 percent of U.S. residents say that walkability is a top priority or a high priority when considering where to live. A survey performed by the National Association of Realtors and National Association of Home Builders (2002) found that greenway trails are the second most important community amenity that potential homeowners cite when choosing a new community. Such home-buyer preferences frequently translate into increased property values and enhanced tax revenue for communities that incorporate greenway trails into planning. Nicholls and Crompton (2005) studied the difference in property values and subsequent property tax revenue attributable to a greenway trail in Austin, Texas. A trail called Barton Creek Greenbelt begins near downtown Austin and follows a creek for 7.9 miles. It is used by mountain bikers and hikers and provides access for rock climbing and swimming. The study found that neighborhoods with access to and views of the trail command higher property values and that these higher property values generate additional tax revenue for municipal and county governments (Nicholls and Crompton 2005). In the Barton neighborhood, properties close to the trail had a $44,332 (20 percent of mean sales price) premium. In the Travis neighborhood, properties adjacent to the trail fetched a $14,777 (6 percent of mean sales price) premium. Nicholls and Crompton (2005) estimate the city received approximately $59,000 per year in taxes due to increased property values near the trail in the Barton and Travis neighborhoods. This amounted to approximately 5 percent of the city's annual debt payments of $1.1 million for the original land purchase and trail development. Although the additional tax revenue from these neighborhoods does not compensate for the trail's expense, the authors point out that many more Austin residents and visitors use the trail than just its neighbors. For a highly valued community-wide resource such as the Barton Creek Greenbelt, the benefits will accrue far beyond the immediate neighborhoods.

A 1990s study examined the selling prices for homes in three neighborhoods in Windsor, Ontario, across the Detroit River from Detroit, in relationship to proximity to greenway and greenspace. This study found that the closer a property is to a natural area or greenway, the higher its value increases, which results in higher tax revenue for the municipality (Zegarac and Muir 1996).

In summary, like a magnificent gem on display, greenway trails attract visitors from near and far. In general, it is fair to say that greenways generate revenues and jobs, help reduce the cost of public services, add value to the landscape and improve the value of surrounding property, and offer an excellent long-term return on investment.

Economic Benefits of Canoeing and Kayaking

Kayakers, canoers, and other paddlers contribute a significant amount of money to local economies. Through spending money on equipment, gas, food, lodging, and other items paddlers provide revenue to local communities.

In 2011, outdoor recreation participants in water sports (including paddling, but excluding fishing and hunting) spent $19.4 billion on gear, accessories, and vehicles, and another $66.8 billion on trip-related purchases, totaling $86.2 billion. These expenditures of $86.2 billion supported 802,062 jobs and provided $8.6 billion in federal, state, and local tax revenues. If the ripple effect is considered, which estimates the impacts of spending, jobs, and wages as they circulate further through the economy, this multiplier-effect spending is estimated to be $206.3 billion, 1,521,486 additional jobs, and $20.8 billion in additional federal, state, and local tax revenues (Outdoor Industry Association 2012). Earlier research had shown that 23.6 million people in the United States or 11 percent of the population participate in paddle-based recreation and that this recreation industry contributes $36.1 billion annually to the U.S. economy (Outdoor Industry Foundation 2006).

Paddling access to waters adjacent to the Detroit RiverWalk is currently provided at Belle Isle Beach, Milliken State Park, and Maheras-Gentry Park. Paddlers can launch at any one of these three locations and enjoy the Detroit RiverWalk from a water perspective. Currently there are at least three businesses supporting kayaking in the Detroit River along the Detroit RiverWalk: Detroit River Sports, Riverside Kayak Connection, and Honest John's Bar and Grill that does kayak tours.

Economic Benefits of Fishing

Throughout the United States, fishing is big business. U.S. Department of the Interior, U.S. Fish and Wildlife Service, U.S. Department of Commerce, and U.S. Census Bureau (2011) have shown that in 2011, 33.1 million U.S. residents sixteen years old and older enjoyed a variety of fishing opportunities throughout the country. Anglers fished 554 million days and took 455 million fishing trips. They spent $41.8 billion in fishing-related expenses during the year (U.S. Department of the Interior, U.S. Fish and Wildlife Service, U.S. Department of Commerce, and U.S. Census Bureau 2011). Freshwater anglers numbered 27.5 million. They fished 456 million days and took 369 million trips to freshwater in 2011. Freshwater anglers spent $25.7 billion on freshwater fishing trips and equipment. According to the Michigan Department of Natural Resources, Michigan anglers spent $2.4 billion in trip-related expenses and equipment in 2011.

Clearly, fishing is economically important on the Detroit River. Each spring we experience March Madness, but I am not talking about basketball. Nearly ten million walleye ascend the Detroit River from Lake Erie to spawn, attracting thousands of anglers and national and international fishing tournaments. These fishing tournaments have landed many 13–14 pound walleye. Anglers from all over North America come to the Detroit River because of both the numbers and size of walleye.

Walleye are caught throughout the entire Detroit River, considered part of the "Walleye Capital of the World." To capture, organize, and celebrate this "walleye fever," Downriver Walleye Federation was established to unite walleye fishermen that ply the Detroit River and Lake Erie. The club's primary goal is to exchange ideas and information about walleye fishing on the Detroit River and Lake Erie. Downriver Walleye Federation convenes monthly meetings that attract over one hundred anglers and include engaging speakers. Throughout the year, members compete against each other in walleye tournaments. Tournament fees are very low, and competition is high. Club members have substantial experience in river jigging and hand line trolling, and members are willing to share their fishing expertise with all. It should be no surprise that walleye fishing on the Michigan side of the lower Detroit River alone brings in more than $1 million to local communities each spring.

This world-class walleye fishery also attracts professional tournaments. FLW Outdoors has frequently held walleye tournaments on the Detroit River offering over $500,000 in prize money. In 2007, U.S. Fish and Wildlife Service, Metropolitan Affairs Coalition, the Detroit Metro Sports Commission, Detroit Metro Convention & Visitors Bureau, and the City of Detroit Mayor's Office worked with FLW Outdoors to bring the Chevy Open bass fishing tournament to the Detroit River and western Lake Erie. Over two hundred professional and two hundred amateur anglers participated in a four-day bass tournament that offered $1.5 million in prize money. This Chevy Open also generated an additional $4–5 million in the economy related to lodging, fuel, food, equipment, etc.

Economic Benefits of Birding

Interest in bird watching is growing worldwide and even along the Detroit River. The economic significance of this outdoor recreational pastime in 2011 was that 71.8 million wildlife watchers in the United States spent $54.9 billion on their wildlife-watching activities around their homes and on trips away from their homes (U.S. Department of the Interior, U.S. Fish and Wildlife Service, U.S. Department of Commerce, and U.S. Census Bureau 2011).

According to a U.S. Department of the Interior, U.S. Fish and Wildlife Service, U.S. Department of Commerce, and U.S. Census Bureau (2011) study, nearly a third of the U.S. population enjoyed wildlife watching in 2011. For this study, wildlife watching was defined as closely observing, feeding, and photographing wildlife, visiting public parks around the home because of wildlife, and maintaining plantings and natural areas around the home for the benefit of wildlife.

This study found that during 2011, 71.8 million U.S. residents, 30 percent of the U.S. population sixteen years old or older, participated in wildlife-watching activities (U.S. Department of the Interior, U.S. Fish and Wildlife Service, U.S. Department of Commerce, and U.S. Census Bureau 2011). People who took an interest in wildlife around their homes numbered 68.6 million, while those who took trips away from their homes to wildlife watch numbered 22.5 million people.

Of all the wildlife observed for recreation in the United States, birds attracted the greatest following. Approximately 46.7 million people observed birds around the home and on trips in 2011 (U.S. Department of the Interior, U.S. Fish and Wildlife Service, U.S. Department of Commerce, and U.S. Census Bureau 2011). A large majority, 88 percent or 41.3 million people, observed birds around the home, while 38 percent or 17.8 million people, took trips away from home to go bird watching. Participants averaged 110 days of birding in 2011.

Detroit Audubon Society has recorded over three hundred fifty species of birds in the Detroit River corridor. The Detroit RiverWalk offers outstanding birding at the far eastern end in Belle Isle State Park—the crown-jewel of the RiverWalk necklace. Belle Isle is one of the only remaining forested areas along this now urban-industrial corridor and is Detroit's version of New York's Central Park. During the winter is an excellent time to see waterfowl, and during the spring and fall you can experience the songbird migration. The birding checklist for this 980-acre island park alone boasts 232 species. Entry-level birding experiences on the Detroit RiverWalk can be obtained at a birding station at Gabriel Richard Park that features four spotting scopes, an interpretive panel, and quarterly programming offered by Detroit Audubon Society and U.S. Fish and Wildlife Service, and at Milliken State Park.

Economic Benefits of Boating

Economic studies show that boating on the Great Lakes is big business. According to U.S. Coast Guard data, there are 4.3 million boats registered in the eight Great Lakes states, representing one third of all registered boats in the United States (Great Lakes Commission 2007). Spending on boats and boating activities in the Great Lakes states totaled nearly $16 billion in 2003, directly supporting 107,000 jobs (Great Lakes Commission 2007). When secondary effects were factored in, the total job number grew to 244,000, with economic impacts of $19 billion in sales, $6.4 billion in personal income, and $9.2 billion in additional value-added benefits. Beneficiaries of this activity included manufacturers, retailers, marinas, restaurants, lodging accommodations, charter operators, and other businesses largely concentrated near docking facilities. Michigan, with its considerable Great Lakes coastline, led the region with nearly one million recreational boats, 42 percent of which belonged to residents of its coastal counties.

Michigan ranks third in the nation for boat registrations and for boat sales (National Marine Manufacturers Association 2014). Approximately 21 percent of Michigan's boats are registered in Wayne (which includes the Detroit River), Oakland, and Macomb counties. According to the National Marine Manufacturers Association (2014), boating contributed $7.4 billion to Michigan's economy in 2012, including 39,746 jobs and 1,404 businesses.

Boating access from the Detroit RiverWalk is available from Milliken State Park and Marina. This marina has thirty-five transient slips and sixteen seasonal slips and is operational from April 30 to October 2 for overnight boating.

Economic Benefits of Hunting

First and foremost, it should be noted that no hunting occurs along the Detroit RiverWalk. However, you might be surprised to learn that Ducks Unlimited has identified the metropolitan region of Detroit as being one of the top ten metropolitan areas for waterfowl hunting in the United States and outstanding waterfowl hunting (i.e., duck and goose) opportunities are available in the lower Detroit River and western Lake Erie (Card 2013). As waterfowl migrate from the Arctic Circle and Canada to their overwintering grounds in the Caribbean and Gulf of Mexico they need places to stop, rest, and feed. These waterfowl, often in tens to hundreds of thousands, come to stopover habitats along the Detroit River and western Lake Erie that provide food and an opportunity to rest. Most are attracted by rich beds of wild celery and other food in the Detroit River. It almost seems paradoxical to sometimes see this number of waterfowl staging and feeding in the shadow of big industry along the Detroit River. It is even more amazing, near the mouth of the Detroit River, to see them lift off the water in such density that they sometimes blacken the sky. These transcontinental waterfowl migrations are clearly one of nature's great spectacles.

Waterfowl hunting is most common around the islands and in the marshes of the lower Detroit River and western Lake Erie. Good examples include certain units of the Detroit River International Wildlife Refuge, Pointe Mouillee State Game Area, and Erie State Game Area. Again, no waterfowl hunting occurs along the Detroit RiverWalk. In the lower Detroit River, the Gibraltar Duck Hunter's Association even hosts a youth duck hunt each year to allow over fifty young boys and girls to go waterfowl hunting with a seasoned hunter. This event is held each year to help promote and sustain the hunting tradition in southeast Michigan.

According to the U.S. Department of the Interior, U.S. Fish and Wildlife Service, U.S. Department of Commerce, and U.S. Census Bureau (2011), 13.7 million people sixteen years old and older enjoyed hunting a variety of animals within the United States in 2011. These individuals hunted 282 million days and took 257 million trips. Hunting expenditures totaled $33.7 billion. In Michigan alone, hunting has had a $2.3 billion economic impact, including expenses related to food and lodging, and $1.3 billion spent on equipment.

In 2011, 2.6 million migratory bird hunters devoted twenty-three million days on twenty-one million trips for hunting birds such as ducks, geese, and doves (U.S. Department of the Interior, U.S. Fish and Wildlife Service, U.S. Department of Commerce, and U.S. Census Bureau 2011). Hunters averaged nine days per year pursuing migratory birds. Migratory bird-related spending for trips and equipment was $1.8 billion in 2011. Of this amount, $942 million was spent on hunting trips. An estimated $316 million or 34 percent of all trip expenditures were on food and lodging, and $390 million (41 percent) were on transportation. Such close-to-home hunting opportunities clearly help support metropolitan Detroit's outdoor recreational economy.

Concluding Remarks

Detroit, considered part of the industrial heartland and Rust Belt, was the butt of jokes for decades. But a revival is now underway in surprising ways as new businesses attract young professionals. The Detroit RiverFront Conservancy and its partners are improving close-to-home, outdoor recreation and improving quality-of-life in a fashion that helps attract and retain employees for business. Such efforts are realizing surprising return on investments and have the potential to return even more in the future. With metropolitan Detroit's continentally significant natural resources and concomitant outdoor recreational assets like the Detroit RiverWalk, the Dequindre Cut, other greenway trails, the Detroit Heritage River Water Trail, Byways to Flyways Bird Driving Tour, and nationally recognized fishing, boating, and hunting, Detroit has the potential to considerably expand its outdoor recreational economy and help become a more sustainable city. That, in turn, can help Michigan become a top-ten natural resource economy state.

CHAPTER 8

Why Care about the Revitalization of Detroit?

I t would be easy to be negative or even cynical about the socioeconomic hardships and challenges of Detroit. Detroit has experienced over a 60 percent decline in population since 1950 and a considerable loss of industry. During this time period Detroit also experienced rising unemployment, increased cost of living, decreased access to city services, racial unrest (e.g., 1967 riots), and increased crime. In 2015, 40.3 percent of its population lived below the poverty level and the per capita income was $15,038 or 57 percent of the Michigan state average (U.S. Census Bureau 2015). To many, Detroit became the embodiment of the Rust Belt. The decline of population, industry, and jobs, and manifestation of other socioeconomic problems, culminated in 2013 with largest municipal bankruptcy filing in the United States, by debt, estimated at $18–20 billion.

Some will say that the problems of Detroit are just too great to solve, that the amount of resources and time it will take to fix these problems are just too great. The purpose of this chapter is to provide some compelling reasons for people to care about the revitalization of Detroit. In essence, this chapter is asking you to think again about Detroit and what its revitalization means to not only the city, but the United States and world. For organizational purposes, this discussion will be divided into three primary reasons to care about the revitalization of Detroit: cities are the creative engines that drive innovation and growth; it is an economic and political fact that we are all inextricably linked and that Detroit is an indispensable part of the American economy and culture; and Detroit has always been there to help meet the needs of the nation and world, and now Detroit needs the nation to help Detroit create the America for tomorrow. Clearly, there are other reasons, but it is hoped that these three will help you perhaps reconsider your understanding and perceptions of the importance of the revitalization of Detroit.

Cities Are the Creative Engines that Drive Innovation and Growth

Cities have been engines of innovation since Plato and Socrates debated in the marketplace of Athens. Today, not only do 80 percent of all U.S. citizens live in cities, but in 2010 almost 85 percent of the U.S. gross domestic product was generated by 259 large cites, and by 2025 more than 10 percent of the global gross domestic product growth will come from large U.S. cities (McKinsey Global Institute 2012). Today, it is generally accepted that goods and services are produced most efficiently in densely populated areas that provide access to a pool of skilled labor, a network of complementary firms that act as suppliers, and a critical mass of customers. Much of the manufacturing and service sectors of the economy is typically concentrated in cities, where they benefit from agglomeration economies and ample markets for inputs, outputs, and labor, and where ideas and knowledge are rapidly diffused.

There is no doubt that healthy, dynamic cities are an integral part of sustained economic growth. The World Bank (1998) has shown that as countries develop, cities account for an ever-increasing share of national income: urban areas generate 55 percent of gross national product in low-income countries; 73 percent in middle-income countries; and 85 percent in high-income countries.

Today, cities can be centers of synergistic collaboration that can catalyze innovation and growth. Cities enable people to learn from each other. Large populations of urban dwellers increase the potential for collaboration, which in turn can lead to greater creativity and innovation. In essence, cities can be unique by leveraging the human capital in a collaborative and synergistic fashion to spark creativity and innovation. Indeed, many of the great human inventions have been made in a collaborative and synergistic fashion, from Athenian philosophy to Henry Ford's Model Ts to the Internet. The Detroit history of Henry Ford is a good example of leveraging the talent in cities to create inventions that warrants further elaboration.

Detroit's strategic location at the heart of the Great Lakes and ready access to wood and iron ore, and the pressing need to move people and goods by water, allowed it to become a leader in shipbuilding. However, it was also the creative talent found in Detroit and the synergy among the members of that talent pool that propelled Detroit to become a center of innovation of iron shipbuilding and maritime engineering. For example, the Detroit Dry Dock Company was incorporated in 1872 and grew into one of the most important shipbuilders in the Great Lakes to meet this maritime need to move people and goods (Glaeser 2011). Detroit's prowess in shipbuilding climaxed in the 1890s when more ships were built along the Detroit River than any other city in America.

From 1880 to 1882 Henry Ford served as an apprentice machinist at the Detroit Dry Dock Company. That experience gave Ford his first exposure to technologically sophisticated engine production (Glaeser 2011). Demonstrated expertise in building carriages and building and repairing ship engines would make Detroit a natural place to build automobiles.

In 1908, Henry Ford and his colleagues introduced the Model T as a simple, sturdy, and relatively inexpensive motorcar for "the great multitude." In 1913, Henry Ford went on to install the first moving assembly line for the mass production of automobiles. This innovation reduced the time it took to build a car from more than twelve hours to two hours and thirty minutes. Clearly, this creativity and these innovations were made possible by the talent of Detroit and the synergy created within that pool of talent.

Another more recent good example of synergistic collaboration in Detroit is the catalyzing innovation and economic development work of Dan Gilbert. Dan Gilbert is a multibillionaire who is chairman and founder of Rock Ventures and Quicken Loans. Today, Gilbert and his partners own or control through leases ninety properties in downtown Detroit, including much of the retail space along Woodward Avenue in the core of downtown.

Gilbert's efforts are strategically geared toward making Detroit America's smartest urban investment by creating a technology and entertainment hub in the Motor City. Gilbert is relying on his wealth and associations to create the critical mass of commercial businesses that will attract other start-ups away from New York, Chicago, and Silicon Valley. Gilbert's total investment in Detroit as of 2017 is $2.2 billion. As part of this investment he has renovated more than eighty-five commercial properties accounting for more than fourteen million square feet in the city's urban core. He constantly promotes Detroit with any and all businesses and the media and is evangelical about the importance of creating spaces that draw foot traffic in the downtown and Midtown neighborhoods of Detroit (Alberta 2014).

Gilbert, who was born and raised in metropolitan Detroit and whose father and grandfather were born and worked in Detroit, cares passionately about Detroit but also sees it as a smart economic investment. His plans, according to Brent D. Ryan, author of *Design after Decline: How America Rebuilds Shrinking Cites,* amount to one of the most ambitious privately financed urban reclamation projects in American history (Ryan 2012). Opportunity Detroit, as Gilbert has branded it, is both a rescue mission for the city of Detroit and a business venture. Gilbert has noted:

> I am certain Detroit and Detroiters will bring their best game and show the rest of the world what we are capable of achieving. There is no doubt that if we work together and open ourselves up to the creative ideas and exciting opportunities all around us, Detroit will inspire people from within and beyond its borders to transform our city into one of the biggest success stories of the twenty-first century. (Pinho 2014, 1)

A second example of synergistic business collaboration benefiting Detroit has been the work of the late Mike Illich, a Detroit entrepreneur and owner of the international fast food franchise Little Caesars Pizza, the Detroit Red Wings, the Detroit Tigers, the Fox Theatre, and more. Recently, Illich Holdings completed a new $863 million Detroit Red Wings hockey and basketball arena, called Little Caesars Arena, off Woodward Avenue in the central business and entertainment district, and has worked with Wayne State University to build an adjacent $50 million, 120,000-square-foot Mike Illich School of Business. These developments are helping to create a unique destination to live, work, and play and to enjoy professional sports and entertainment alongside restaurants, shops, office spaces, and downtown housing.

A third example of synergistic collaboration is the work of Roger Penske, a metropolitan Detroit entrepreneur who has been extensively involved in professional automobile racing. For example, his auto-racing team, Team Penske, holds more victories than any other owner in the Indianapolis 500—sixteen victories. He is also owner of Penske Corporation and other automotive-related industries. Penske cares deeply about Detroit and championed bringing Super Bowl XL to Detroit in 2006 and making the Belle Isle Grand Prix a showpiece on the North American racing circuit. He also played a key leadership role by serving as chairman of the board for the QLINE streetcar vehicle project that is transforming downtown Detroit, and much more. Clearly, Gilbert, Illich, and Penske are good current examples of catalyzing economic development in Detroit that will pay long-term benefits. However, it would be remiss to not mention the leadership of Detroit mayor Mike Duggan, who must be applauded for the changes he has brought and the emphasis his team has placed on an equitable recovery, and the important contributions of faith-based organizations. Clearly, Detroit churches, synagogues, mosques, and other faith-based organizations are playing critical roles in strengthening the community, including providing food, clothing, and shelter for those in need and in community development and housing programs.

Today, Detroit is at the forefront of what sociologists call a postindustrial society—where the service sector begins to generate more wealth than the manufacturing sector. Many, like Gilbert, Illich, and Penske, have felt that Detroit is alive with visions, ideas, plans, and action for revitalization, including JPMorgan Chase that played a supportive role. For example, in 2014, JPMorgan Chase pledged $100 million over five years to help accelerate Detroit's recovery. The rationale for this major commitment was that JPMorgan Chase had been doing business in Detroit for more than eighty years and that the company believed in its future. JPMorgan Chase saw hardworking leaders who put aside partisanship to focus on problem solving. They saw committed nonprofit organizations and businesses with deep roots in the community. Drawing on JPMorgan Chase's global experience serving clients and communities, the company saw an opportunity to do more to help accelerate Detroit's recovery. JPMorgan Chase had worked closely with Detroit's leaders to understand their priorities and how to support their efforts, and the five-year $100 million commitment was developed to be both responsive to Detroit's needs and consistent with JPMorgan Chase's core strengths.

In a September 16, 2015, opinion/editorial in the *Wall Street Journal* titled "How to Rev the Growth Engine," JPMorgan Chase chairman and CEO Jamie Dimon noted:

> I've traveled to Detroit on business for more than 25 years, and the signs of the city's recovery are becoming apparent. Although the city has a long way to go, you can feel the increasing energy and spirit of cooperation that businesses, government and nonprofits have to increase economic growth and create greater opportunity for all. The city has exited bankruptcy, fixed thousands of streetlights, and improved emergency response times and started to reduce blight.

In a September 2015 *Meet the Press* interview, Dimon noted, "Detroit is a sign of hope for America." In that interview, *Meet the Press* moderator Chuck Todd agreed and noted, "The nation wants to save Detroit. You can feel it. It's bipartisan."

Edward Glaeser, an economics professor at Harvard University and the author of *Triumph of the City*, calls cities our "greatest invention" (Glaeser 2011). Glaeser argues that the city allows for an easier exchange of ideas, which leads to innovation. Cities enable their citizens to learn from one another and to become better, in a sense, through collaboration of talented individuals colocated in one place. Cities facilitate exchange of ideas and can create a synergy where something magical can happen that leads to innovation and growth.

Much attention is currently being paid to cities because 60 percent of the world's population will be living in them by 2030 (United Nations 2006; Haub 2007). Clearly, much must be done to harness the city and all its energy toward economic and social development. This has been acknowledged by the United Nations Department of Economic and Social Affairs, Population Division (2014, 1) in its *World Urbanization Prospects* report stating: "As the world continues to urbanize, sustainable development challenges will be increasingly concentrated in cities."

Knowledge-based innovation is the critical ingredient for prosperity and well-being in the twenty-first century, and it thrives in local spaces that cluster economic producers, value diverse ideas and cultures, and include all residents in learning opportunities (Bradford 2002). If cities are designed properly and managed effectively, they can become breeding grounds for innovation and creativity. They increase interactions among diverse stakeholders, increasing the likelihood of generating creative ideas and solutions. Cities both bring people together who share similar interests and cultural norms, and improve synergistic collaboration by decreasing transactional costs through provision of transit systems, meeting places, and other forms of infrastructure. In short, cities can be power plants of human energy and creativity.

In today's information economy, knowledge and creativity are increasingly recognized as key strategic assets and powerful engines that drive economic growth (Baycan 2011). Indeed, Florida (2002), in his book *The Rise of the Creative Class: And How It's Transforming Work, Leisure, Community and Everyday Life*, has documented the importance of creative cities. He focuses on the importance of combining artistic or cultural creativity with business entrepreneurship and technological innovation. The resulting synergies, he argues, are the key to prosperity in an age of knowledge-based production. Florida argues that the key to economic growth lies not just in the ability to attract the creative class, but to translate that underlying advantage into creative economic outcomes in the form of new ideas, new high-tech businesses, and regional growth. Bradford (2004) has shown that cities have become strategic sites for creativity and growth, as they represent the ideal scale for the intensive, face-to-face interactions that generate the new ideas that power knowledge-based innovation. Clearly, cities like Detroit that have long histories of creativity and innovation clearly warrant our attention because they hold much promise to achieving our long-term goal of sustainable development.

Detroit Is an Indispensable Part of the American Economy and Culture

It is hard for most people to really know how wealthy Detroit was during the early automotive years. During that time Detroit could probably best be described as the Silicon Valley of its day. Entrepreneurs flocked to Detroit because it was at the cutting edge of industrial innovation. The assembly line, perfected by Henry Ford, launched a whole new mode of production that revolutionized the world. The city was a magnet for migrants pursuing the American Dream, and in the 1920s Detroit was one of the fastest growing cities in the world. Then Detroit flexed its industrial might during World War II and became the arsenal of democracy and the center of the greatest concentration of applied science and technology the world had ever seen. Clearly, Detroit was the flagship of America's industrial power.

From that history, it is easy to argue that Detroit has, at certain times in its history, been ahead of the curve and a pioneer. It was the first city to perfect the assembly line, the first city to enable working-class families to climb to the ranks of the middle class, the first city to go through suburban expansion based on the automobile, and the first city to truly feel the full effects of deindustrialization.

It is important to note that today Detroit is still a force in the U.S. economy. For example, the American Automotive Policy Council has shown that General Motors Corporation, Ford Motor Company, and Fiat Chrysler Automobiles, and their suppliers, are currently responsible for 3 percent of the U.S. economy and provide the largest source of manufacturing jobs. Matt Blunt, the former governor of Missouri and president of the American Automobile Policy Council notes: "American automakers drive the U.S. economy and their investments are making America more competitive in a global economy, and making significant contributions to the revival of manufacturing here in America" (2015). According to the American Automotive Policy Council, Fiat Chrysler

U.S., Ford, and General Motors, which are headquartered in the Detroit metropolitan area, operate more than two hundred assembly plants, factories, research labs, and other automotive facilities across thirty-two states in the nation. Over the past five years, these three leading U.S. automakers have exported more than $637 billion in vehicles and parts and invest around $18 billion in research and development annually (2015).

But Detroit is much more than the automobile capital of the United States; it is also a center for arts and culture. The great diversity of the city and its metropolitan region has yielded a rich cultural fabric. This Detroit culture has influenced both American and global culture through its commercial enterprises and various forms of popular music throughout the twentieth and twenty-first centuries. From the Motown Sound and rhythm and blues to techno and hip-hop, its music has impacted the nation and world. Detroit's musical legacy is celebrated at Hitsville USA, the home of Motown Music, as well as at the jazz clubs, techno clubs, and other musical venues throughout the city. Detroit is home to the second largest theater district in the United States, including great masterpieces like the Fox Theatre (the first Fox theater built in the 1920s and the first theater to have live sound), Masonic Temple Theatre (the largest building of its kind in the world built in the 1920s), Detroit Opera House that is home to the Michigan Opera Theatre (originally opened in 1922 as the fifth largest theater in the world), Fillmore Theatre (built in 1925 as a movie house in the Renaissance revival style of architecture), and Orchestra Hall (built in 1919 and internationally renowned for its acoustic qualities), home to the Detroit Symphony Orchestra (the fourth oldest orchestra in the United States).

Detroit's Midtown is known as the cultural center of the city because it has numerous cultural icons colocated within walking distance in the center of the city. Development of the cultural center dates back to 1913 as part of the City Beautiful movement that advocated the clustering of important public buildings. Numerous architectural and cultural monuments are found in the Midtown/Cultural Center:

- Detroit Institute of Arts (its collection is among the top six in the United States, comprising a multicultural and multinational survey of human creativity from prehistory through the twenty-first century)
- the main branch of the Detroit Public Library (part of the fourth largest public library system in the United States)
- the Horace H. Rackham Educational Memorial Building (a bold reinterpretation of classical architecture that breaks with tradition while borrowing heavily from the aesthetic of the late art deco period)
- Detroit Historical Museum (over 250,000 artifacts that represent Detroit's more than three-hundred-year history)
- Charles H. Wright Museum of African American History (holds the world's largest permanent exhibit on African American culture)
- Museum of Contemporary Art Detroit (presents art at the forefront of contemporary culture)
- Michigan Science Center (which includes Michigan's only Chrysler IMAX Dome Theatre; the Dassault Systèmes Planetarium; the DTE Energy Sparks Theater; the Chrysler Science Stage; an 8,700-square-foot Science Hall for traveling exhibits, hands-on exhibit galleries focusing on space, life, and physical science; the United States Steel Fun Factory; an exhibit gallery just for children; and more)
- Wayne State University (a nationally recognized metropolitan research institution offering more than 380 academic programs through thirteen schools and colleges to more than twenty-seven thousand students)
- Detroit's College for Creative Studies (a private, fully accredited college that enrolls more than 1,400 students pursuing Bachelor and Master of Fine Arts degrees for successful careers in the dynamic and growing creative industries)

- the Hilberry and Bonstelle Theaters
- numerous art galleries like the Detroit Artists Market, N'Namdi Center for Contemporary Art, Simone DeSousa Gallery, Scarab Club, and more.

Few would question the impact Detroit has had on music. Music has been the dominant feature of Detroit's nightlife for over one hundred years, and there is no doubt that Detroit music has impacted the world. During the 1950s Detroit was well known for jazz when stars of the era came to Detroit's Black Bottom neighborhood to perform. One of the highlights of Detroit's musical history is Motown Records that was an international success during the 1960s and early 1970s. It was founded in Detroit by Berry Gordy Jr. and was home to many popular recording artists, including Marvin Gaye, the Temptations, Stevie Wonder, Diana Ross and the Supremes, and more. It was also during the late 1960s that Detroiter Aretha Franklin became America's preeminent female soul artist.

In the late 1960s, metropolitan Detroit was the epicenter for high-energy rock music by groups like MC5 and Iggy and the Stooges, precursors of the punk rock movement. Rock acts from southeast Michigan that enjoyed much success in the 1970s included Bob Seger, Ted Nugent and the Amboy Dukes, Alice Cooper, the Romantics, and Grand Funk Railroad. More recent popular rock/pop music artists include Marshall Crenshaw, Kid Rock, Jack White and the White Stripes, the Von Bondies, Madonna, and more.

The Detroit area is well known as the birthplace of the techno movement that has grown from local radio and clubs to dance venues worldwide. People from all over the world attend Detroit's annual Movement Electronic Music Festival held on Memorial Day weekend. Hip-hop rose to prominence in the late 1990s with the emergence of Detroit rap artists like Eminem.

One truism today is that we are all inextricably linked on a global scale. Another one is that Detroit is an indispensable part of the American

TABLE 11. Quotes on Why Detroit Matters

QUOTE	INDIVIDUAL
Detroit is the heartbeat of America and the world!	Hubert Massey, *master muralist/artist, Kresge Fine Arts Fellow*
Detroit is the heart of a region that is four million strong, with each and every person carrying a portion of the city's soul—past, present, and future. Its history is the history of twentieth-century America, with cultural institutions that are among the nation's treasures, an architectural legacy that is unique among American cities, and a spirit that is indomitable. It was creative thinking that built this region, and creative thinking will sustain it.	Rip Rapson, *president and chief executive officer, the Kresge Foundation*
Detroit matters because it is the heart and soul of the working people of America, and every genre of music from gospel to jazz, pop and rock to hip-hop flourishes and is nurtured here.	Joan Belgrave, *singer, songwriter, producer*
Detroit has changed your world in more ways than you can count. The assembly line, eventually giving us the arsenal of democracy. Motown, an attempt to bring assembly-line production methods to pop music, essentially becoming a factory for making hit records, in the process altering the course of Western Civilization . . . and when all of the above was gone, leaving Detroit a company town with no company, Detroit techno rose from the desolation to change the course of civilization again. Detroit's motto is Resurget cineribus which means "We will rise from the ashes." Res ipsa loquitur.	Mick Collins, *singer, songwriter, musician—the Dirtbombs, the Gories*
Detroit matters because, whatever the circumstances, its creativity never ceases.	Graham W. J. Beal, *former director, president, and CEO, Detroit Institute of Arts*
Detroit—from the expanding U.S. frontier to the birth of the Industrial Revolution, to the arsenal of democracy, to the sound track of the civil rights movement—has been at the center of the American experience. We are the tough, gritty, tenacious, and hard working. Detroiters are builders, engineers, and artists; makers of things and writers of songs. Detroit matters because Detroit represents the creative ingenuity that is the basis of American resilience.	Matt Seeger, *professor of communication and dean of the College of Fine, Performing and Communication Arts, Wayne State University*

Detroit matters because it's where I'm from and even in the wake of the bankruptcy it stands as a cultural beacon and will never be bankrupt of culture, soul, and spirit!!	James Carter, *world-renowned jazz saxophone player*
Detroit matters as a contemporary illustration of how democracy cannot be assumed a right but rather a privilege to be earned by creative and intelligent citizens, including those in the artistic community, who nurture it responsibly or it decays.	Douglas Stratton, *Detroit philanthropist and founder of the Stratton Foundation*
What is special about Detroit, and the other cities like it, is the perseverance and courage of its citizens to overcome the policies and still strive to believe in the American dream.	Mitch Ryder, *singer, songwriter, Detroit rock-and-roll icon*
Detroit is one of the most interesting cities in the world because it's evolving in front of your eyes into what it will be in its next act. It was at the forefront of the industrial age in the last century, and it won't be ignored in this century either.	Karla Murray, *national manager at Film Detroit (Detroit Film Office)*
Detroit is this wonderfully unique stew of people, music, and culture. Notice that I didn't say a "melting pot." What makes Detroit cool is that each culture is represented in the stew and each flavor is distinct but complementary. There's nowhere else quite like it.	Rev. Robert Jones Sr., *acclaimed roots musician, artist, storyteller, teacher, and preacher*
Detroit is humanity—in all its beauty, ugliness, spirit, struggle, injury, hope, despair, tragedy, love, hate, history. Detroit makes you humble. Detroit makes you real. Detroit is a provocative piece of art that won't allow you to remain untouched, callous, or disengaged. Detroit makes you love it and work harder for it than you've worked for anything in your life.	Sarah James, *fundraising and membership chair for People for Palmer Park, and communications chair for University District Community Association*
The hardships that we've experienced have not only required an environment of innovation, they've bred a culture of passionate expression and creative ingenuity. We know what it is to fight for our art, and because of that the things we create are shaping the way creators and collectors view the world.	Sara Frey, *strategist at Skidmore Studio, cofounder of Free Art Friday Detroit*
Detroit isn't a city on the verge of collapse. It's a city on the verge of transformation. Students who study here can take part in the reinvention of the American city. It's an unprecedented opportunity.	M. Roy Wilson, MD, *president, Wayne State University*
Because it's big enough to matter in the world, but small enough that you can matter in it.	Jeanette Pierce, *D:hive*

Detroiters were born with wings. Our wings have a deep history. Our roads paved the way for every future highway of tomorrow. An international hub full of vitality—of Michigan strength. From the global reach of techno and Motown to the powerful roar of our engines. From style trends to technology, Detroit is the starting line of the world's imagination.	Jessica Care Moore, *poet*

SOURCES: ALL QUOTES ARE TAKEN FROM HARDIN (2013), WITH THE EXCEPTION OF JENNETTE PIERCE QUOTE THAT IS FROM KURAS (2014) AND THE JESSICA CARE MOORE QUOTE THAT IS FROM THE "MOVE THE WORLD" VIDEO PRODUCED AS PART OF DETROIT'S APPLICATION FOR THE SECOND AMAZON HEADQUARTERS (HTTPS://WWW.MLIVE.COM/NEWS/DETROIT/INDEX.SSF/2017/10/DETROIT_PROPELS_MOVE_THE_WORLD.HTML).

economy and culture, and it has and continues to impact the world through technological developments and culture. Detroit clearly matters on a national and international scale. To help put Detroit into a larger perspective, table 11 presents quotes from selected Detroiters on why Detroit matters.

Meeting the Needs of the Nation and World, and Helping Create the America for Tomorrow

When European fashion demanded furs during the 1600s and 1700s, Detroit responded by becoming a leading processor and exporter during the fur trade era. When African American slaves needed help with safe passage through the Underground Railroad during the 1800s, Detroit responded by helping over forty thousand freedom seekers cross the Detroit River and gain their freedom. When the nation called during the Civil War in 1861, Detroiters left their jobs, homes, and loved ones to help save the Union and help emancipate four million African American slaves. When the nation needed help with transporting people and goods as part of settling the west in the 1800s, Detroit became one of the greatest shipbuilding ports in the United States. When the nation needed a means of more efficient land transportation in the early 1900s, Detroit responded by becoming the Motor City and one of the largest industrial manufacturing centers in the world. When the nation needed to supply Europe with the implements of war during World War II, Detroit responded by becoming the "arsenal of democracy" and the leading supplier of military goods in the United States. When the nation needed leaders of the civil rights movement, Detroit citizens stood up and spoke out for racial equality and civil rights. When the nation needed an example of providing affordable housing during the twentieth century, Detroit responded by becoming a beacon of home ownership for the middle class. Clearly, Detroit has a long history of meeting the needs of the nation and world (table 12).

One could easily argue that Detroit has long had an American identity. An American identity is generally understood to be a set of common values like love of liberty, the pursuit of justice, the urge to invent, the desire for wealth, the drive to explore, the quest for spiritual values, and belief in individual freedom. Throughout its history, Detroit has had an American identity as the "arsenal of democracy," the All-American City (in 1966 Detroit was given an All American City Award by the National Civic League), and the Motor City.

There is no doubt that Detroit, over its history, has helped meet the needs of the nation and world. We now need the nation to help Detroit create the America for tomorrow. It has been suggested that a Detroit renaissance is necessary in helping achieve the American Dream—the ideal that every U.S. citizen should have an equal opportunity to achieve success and prosperity through hard work, determination, and initiative. Until that is done, we can't realize the American Dream. This perspective has been captured succinctly by David Houghton, former president of the National Wildlife Refuge Association:

> Detroit is integral to the American Dream with its long history of ingenuity, can-do spirit, risk taking, and industrial and technological might. Until we see a renaissance of Detroit, we can't fully realize the American Dream.

TABLE 12. Examples of How Detroit Has Impacted the Nation and World

ERA	EXAMPLES OF DETROIT'S IMPACT ON THE U.S. AND WORLD	REFERENCES
Fur Trade	• The lands bordering the Detroit River were prime real estate during the fur trade era of the 1600s and 1700s. The river was vital for transportation and for the numerous beaver living in surrounding areas. • Detroit was literally created in response to European demand for hats made from beaver pelts. • The outpost at Detroit became a strategic move in protecting French trapping interests, and it went on to become a leading processer and exporter of furs during the fur trade era. • In the first half of the eighteenth century, the fur trade dominated Detroit's economy. By the 1750s more than two thousand packs of furs came through Detroit.	Pollock (2013)
Underground Railroad	• During the nineteenth century, Detroit was a pivotal part of the Underground Railroad, an informal network of safe houses and people willing to help runaway enslaved people. • Detroit was considered the principal terminus of the Underground Railroad in the west. • Codenamed Midnight, it was the last place many came before crossing the Detroit River to freedom in Canada. • Detroit's unique geographical location, coupled with its radicalized black community and abolitionist sympathizers, made the city a prime crossing location for freedom seekers. • More than forty thousand freedom seekers from the United States entered Canada across the Detroit River.	Tobin and Jones (2007); Walters (2012)
Civil War	• The American Civil War began on April 12, 1861, with the Battle of Fort Sumpter. On April 15, President Abraham Lincoln issued a call for troops. On April 16, Michigan governor Austin Blair issued a call for a regiment of ten companies to fulfill Michigan's quota. This would require $100,000. Michigan did not have a means of furnishing that amount, but Detroit pledged $50,000.	Castel (1998); Dempsey (2011); Huffman (1951); Taylor (2013)

Civil War (*continued*)	■ The First Michigan Volunteer Infantry Regiment, made up of many from Detroit, was the first western regiment to answer President Lincoln's call for volunteers. When they arrived in Washington, President Lincoln exclaimed, "Thank God for Michigan." ■ Detroit sent over six thousand men into battle when its population was but forty-five thousand. ■ The Twenty-fourth Michigan Infantry, many from Detroit, was organized in Detroit and mustered into federal service on August 15, 1862. It was assigned to the famous Iron Brigade. In the Battle of Gettysburg that resulted in the largest number of casualties in the Civil War and is often described as the war's turning point, the Twenty-fourth Michigan Infantry went into battle with 496 officers and men and sustained 363 casualties (89 killed or mortally wounded, 218 otherwise wounded, and 56 captured). ■ During the Civil War, Detroit also provided supplies and provisions to the Union cause.	Castel (1998); Dempsey (2011); Huffman (1951); Taylor (2013)
Shipbuilding	■ During the late 1700s and 1800s, Detroit became a major center of trade and commerce and an embarkation point for the lands farther west. ■ To meet the pressing demand for transportation of passengers and freight, Detroit became one of the greatest shipbuilding ports in the United States. Hundreds of ships were built along the waterfront. During the 1890s, more ships were built along the Detroit River than any other city in America. Shipbuilding provided jobs and supported families locally, but it also impacted the nation and world through billions of dollars of commerce and trade. ■ From 1801 to 1960 at least 655 ships were built at yards and locations from the lower Rouge River to the mouth of the Detroit River. ■ In 1819 the Detroit River was declared a public highway by act of Congress.	Hartig (2003)
Automobiles	■ Metropolitan Detroit's expertise in building steam engines for ships and practical experience in manufacturing coaches and carriages positioned it well for addressing the automotive paradigm shift.	Detroit Historical Society, Detroit, Michigan

Automobiles (*continued*)	- Detroit's first car company started in 1899. - Henry Ford created more efficient manufacturing systems, including assembly lines. - By 1913 the industry grew to the point where there were forty-three different automobile companies operating in the Detroit metropolitan area. - By 1919, 45 percent of Detroit's 308,520 industrial employees were employed in the automobile industry, and Detroit had become the Motor City and one of the largest industrial manufacturing centers in the world.	Detroit Historical Society, Detroit, Michigan
Arsenal of Democracy	- Following the Japanese attack on Pearl Harbor in 1941, the United States plunged into World War II. - U.S. President Franklin D. Roosevelt had recognized the need to help supply Europe with the implements of war and called for the United States to become the great "arsenal of democracy." - Detroit responded by redeploying its vast industrial capacity to play a critical role in the ultimate Allied victory in 1945. - In 1942, all automobile assembly lines in metropolitan Detroit ceased production of civilian vehicles and manufactured only military vehicles. - In total, metropolitan Detroit companies received contracts worth about $14 billion or 10 percent of all U.S. military output in 1943. - By 1944 metropolitan Detroit was the leading supplier of military goods in the United States. - During 1942–45, metropolitan Detroit produced about $29 billion of military output and employed approximately 610,000 people in military production. - During WWII Detroit was at the center of the greatest concentration of applied science and technology the world had ever seen. Factories broke every previous production record and poured forth a flood of goods, unleashing American productive and technological genius.	Detroit Historical Society, Detroit, Michigan

Concluding Remarks

Detroiters have always kept this country moving. As poet Jessica Care Moore of Detroit has noted: "This is the world's city. Design here, design the world. Build here, you'll build the world. Make here, create the world. Move here, move the world."

It is my hope that the information presented in this chapter will give you pause for thought and will challenge you to think again about Detroit and what its revitalization means not only to Michigan, but to the United States and world. Cities are the creative engines that drive innovation and growth, and Detroit has demonstrated time and again that its creativity, innovation, and work ethic can impact the nation and world. It is also an economic and political fact that we are all inextricably linked and that Detroit is an indispensable part of the American economy and culture. Finally, Detroit has always been there to help meet the needs of the nation and world, and now Detroit needs the nation to help Detroit create the America for tomorrow. Until we see a renaissance of Detroit we cannot fully realize the American Dream.

Signs of hope abound in Detroit, yet clearly much remains to be done—especially in the neighborhoods. Today, the Millennial generation of entrepreneurs is creating a new version of Detroit, a more sustainable one that is not solely reliant on manufacturing. This is being led by young startups and local businesses through public–private partnerships to restore this once iconic city. I challenge you to come and look around this once great city and see for yourself the sweeping young spirit that is infectious and inviting. This spirit is helping transform Detroit using creative ingenuity and doing it in a fashion that will serve as a model of American resilience. Michigan governor Rick Snyder believes that Detroit is on the path to recovery and called Detroit "America's Comeback City." Lonely Planet agrees and ranked Detroit No. 2 on its list of ten best cities to visit throughout the world in 2018.

CHAPTER 9

Lessons Learned and the Future

The Waterfront Center (1999) believes that water is a defining force that fundamentally shapes the character of each place it touches. The Detroit RiverFront Conservancy agrees and is using this as a premise for creating a new riverfront gathering place for people and wildlife as part of an effort to help revitalize the city and help meet the challenge of the sustainability paradigm shift. The Detroit RiverWalk has been described as transformational for the region by cleaning up industrial brownfields, restoring shoreline habitat, creating public access to the Detroit River, and catalyzing economic development. It is one of the largest, by scale, urban waterfront redevelopment projects in the United States (i.e., 5.5 miles in the heart of downtown Detroit). The Detroit RiverWalk clearly provides evidence and gives hope that Detroit has a bright and more sustainable future, but clearly more needs to be done.

The Detroit RiverWalk is also helping change the perception of the region from that of a degraded urban area in the Rust Belt characterized by abandoned industrial brownfields, a polluted river, and a Great Lakes pollution hotspot (the Detroit River is one of forty-three Great Lakes Areas of Concern identified by the United States and Canada) to one of an international, urban leader in reconnecting people to nature, improving quality of life, showcasing sustainable redevelopment, and enhancing economic development and community pride.

Key lessons learned from this transformational project include:

- establishing a common vision;
- recruiting a well-respected champion;
- ensuring broad support from key stakeholder groups;
- establishing a core delivery team, focused on outcomes and success;
- building trust and ensuring cooperative learning;
- adopting a strategic approach to community engagement, creating a connected community;
- evoking a sense of place; and
- measuring and celebrating successes to sustain momentum (table 13).

Such lessons may be useful to other large urban areas throughout the world in their efforts to reconnect people with natural resources and foster a more sustainable future.

For the Detroit RiverWalk to reach its full potential of creating an inviting destination for all, the Detroit RiverFront Conservancy needs to continue to connect the Detroit RiverWalk with everyday uses and users. Jacobs (1961) has warned that a park plopped down out of context that has no relationship to the environment around it will often be a failed park. A diversity of experiences is at the heart of Jacobs's perspective on cities. She believed that the best public spaces need to create a kaleidoscope of different experiences for city dwellers and that this will help give back grace and delight to neighborhoods, instead of vacuity.

TABLE 13. Key Lessons Learned from Building the Detroit RiverWalk and the Detroit River International Wildlife Refuge in Metropolitan Detroit

KEY LESSONS LEARNED	DESCRIPTION/EXAMPLES
Establish Common Vision	A clear and compelling vision is important in any major urban initiative. This vision must be relevant, appealing, and engaging, and must be a picture that all stakeholders can carry in their hearts and minds (Senge 1990). The conservancy's vision of building the Detroit RiverWalk to reconnect Detroiters to their international riverfront was strongly supported by all stakeholders who emphasized creating an inviting destination for all, enhancing Detroit's image to emphasize its iconic, international riverfront, and developing a collective sense of ownership, accessibility, and responsibility for stewardship.
Recruit a Well-Respected Champion	It was important to recruit champions who had respect in the community and could establish a broad coalition, including government buy-in and an ability to survive changes in administrations. Matthew Cullen (champion for the conservancy) had a long-standing career at General Motors Corporation as general manager of Economic Development and Enterprise Services and more recently as president and chief executive officer at Rock Ventures. Cullen was passionate about the RiverWalk, made it a priority in his busy schedule, helped attract other key Detroit leaders, and helped open doors to leverage resources.
Ensure Broad Support from Key Stakeholder Groups	Major urban projects need broad support from many stakeholder groups, including key leaders. Such strong and early support can help establish legitimacy and can help build momentum. Substantial early support was provided by the Kresge Foundation ($50 million to build the Detroit RiverWalk) and General Motors Corporation (who renovated its world headquarters called the Renaissance Center and switched its headquarters' front door from facing inland to facing the Detroit River).
Establish Core Delivery Team, Focused on Outcomes and Success	A core project delivery team was essential to coordinate among partners, keep on schedule, and fulfill commitments. Key staff was recruited from both the public and private sectors to ensure timely delivery of tangible results. If a project required any permits, early efforts were made to ensure that all regulatory agencies were involved up front in the process to ensure buy-in, support for the project, and timely review and approval of permits. Cooperative learning among team members was essential. The conservancy staff worked closely with all partners to deliver projects on time, within budget, and with quality. Capacity building was achieved by a forty-nine-member board of directors who worked closely with staff.

Build Trust and Ensure Cooperative Learning	The Detroit RiverFront Conservancy has a long history of developing effective working relationships built on trust and respect. Trust and respect make public–private partnerships stronger and increase the probability of success. Such processes require an open and inclusive decision-making process, clear roles and responsibilities, and responsiveness/accountability.
Adopt a Strategic Approach to Community Engagement, Creating a Connected Community	From the outset, the Conservancy adopted a philosophy of working with and for citizens and other stakeholder groups. It was important to engage stakeholders where they were at. A common goal was to achieve local ownership of outcomes and deliverables. The Conservancy was very effective in using design charettes and listening sessions to solicit ideas, get buy-in, and ensure local ownership. Substantial resources and time were devoted to ensuring local ownership and to becoming part of the community fabric.
Evoke a Sense of Place	Much like the effort to re-create front porches on houses in cities to encourage a sense of community, the Detroit RiverWalk is a good example of designing and building gathering places for both people and wildlife. Such convivial places can evoke a sense of place. Understanding places and what people want and wildlife need are critical to making a place special or unique and fostering a sense of authentic human attachment and belonging to an ecosystem.
Measure and Celebrate Successes to Sustain Momentum	In major urban initiatives, it is important to build a record of success and celebrate it frequently in a public fashion. Accomplishments and benefits should be recorded in a fashion that is meaningful to the public. The Conservancy has been very effective in using a broad range of media to share accomplishments, tell compelling stories about the project benefits, and involve youth, business leaders, and politicians in celebrating successes.

SOURCE: HARTIG AND WALLACE 2015.

The Benefits of Making Nature Part of Everyday Urban Life

The Detroit RiverFront Conservancy has implemented many ecological projects that encourage reconnecting with nature. First and foremost, the Detroit RiverWalk is a 5.5-mile riverfront greenway trail that has improved public access to the Detroit River and its over 350 species of birds and over 100 species of fish. Other examples of Detroit RiverFront Conservancy projects undertaken that fostered a closer connection with nature include:

- creating substantial riverfront green spaces like at Milliken State Park and Ralph C. Wilson, Jr. Centennial Park;
- implementing five soft shoreline engineering projects that enhanced riparian habitat along the Detroit River;
- incorporating an innovative stormwater treatment system in Milliken State Park;
- achieving LEED-certification of pavilions;
- creating native wildflower gardens on the RiverWalk;
- establishing a native planting site on the Dequindre Cut under the leadership of the Detroit Garden Center;
- planting native trees;
- establishing butterfly gardens and a birding station at Gabriel Richard Park; and
- constructing a landscape labyrinth for interacting with nature.

The benefits of such projects, designed to reconnect people with nature, are many. Fromm (1973) first described the term "biophilia" to mean passionate love of life or living systems. Entomologist and conservationist E.O. Wilson (1984) later introduced and popularized the biophilia hypothesis that purports that there is a genetic basis for humans to connect with nature and other forms of life. That means that humans have an intrinsic, emotional need to connect with nature.

Out of this thinking came the concept of biophilic city. A biophilic city puts nature at the core of its design and planning, not as an afterthought or add-on. It argues that nature is the key to everything that happens in a city. Timothy Beatley, a leading authority on this subject, describes it this way:

A biophilic city is a city abundant with nature, a city that looks for opportunities to repair and restore and creatively insert nature wherever it can. It is an outdoor city, a physically active city, to which residents spend time enjoying the biological magic and wonder around them. In biophilic cites, residents care about nature and work on its behalf locally and globally. (Beatley 2011, 2)

At their core, biophilic cities protect and actively restore biodiversity. You can think of them as green cities that actively connect residents with nature through urban gardening, greenways, place-making for people and wildlife, and more. Timothy Beatley (2011) and the Biophilic Cities Network have championed this concept and encouraged its application on a global scale. The network believes that biophilic cities provide many opportunities to go outside and enjoy nature through strolling, hiking, bicycling, fishing, birding, exploring flora, fauna, and unique natural areas, and just relaxing. They place a high priority on environmental and conservation education, natural resource interpretation, understanding the importance of biodiversity and ecosystem services, and providing many and varied opportunities to learn about and directly experience nature. In a biophilic city there are many opportunities to join with others in citizen science and other ways of learning about, enjoying, connecting with, and stewarding nature. This can be accomplished through a school, church, environmental organization, conservation club, participating in an organized hike or a cleanup day in a city park, or volunteering for natural resource stewardship projects. Biophilic cities invest in the social and physical infrastructure to strengthen the urban connection to and understanding of nature through greenway trails, nature centers, stewardship programs, school- and community-based conservation initiatives, and parks and recreation programs and projects. Biophilic cities also think globally and recognize the importance of actions to limit the impact of resource use on nature and biodiversity beyond their urban borders.

It is also important to note that there is a growing body of research demonstrating the positive influence of nature on human health and well-being. Nature can literally counteract the negative effects of living in cities. For example, cities can be stressful and can work against human well-being. City life is frequently fast-paced. It is no secret that cities are congested and have generally higher levels of air pollution. Cities can also be perceived as being hard, cold, gray, and depressing. A quiet natural spot on the Detroit RiverWalk can be a respite from the stressors of modern city life. Urban green spaces, with native gardens, butterfly gardens, trees, and waterfront vistas, can provide rest and a positive distraction from hectic city life. Feeling safe in nature can also boost well-being.

The Detroit RiverWalk also encourages more active lifestyles. It is well accepted that more active lifestyles combat obesity, improve cardiovascular health, and increase longevity. It is also important to emphasize that evidence of the emotional and psychological benefits of nature is mounting and impressive. For example, Louv (2005) has shown in his book *Last Child in the Woods* that playing, recreating, and learning in nature can help reduce obesity, attention disorders, and depression. By reducing stress, sharpening concentration, and stimulating creative problem-solving, "nature play" is also emerging as a promising therapy for attention-deficit disorder and other childhood maladies (Louv 2005). From a parental perspective, the reasons to take our children outside are simple:

- It makes kids happier.
- It makes kids healthier.
- It makes kids smarter.
- It's free.
- It's fun for the entire family.

Such evidence provides compelling rationale to complete and even extend the Detroit RiverWalk, expand outdoor recreational opportunities along it, and expand programming that connects families with nature along the RiverWalk.

Whether it's walking, jogging, yoga on the riverfront, Kids Fishing Fest, birding, Reading & Rhythm on the Riverfront, learning through environmental education, art contests, environmental interpretation, or just plain exploring the wetlands of Milliken State Park or the butterfly gardens of Gabriel Richard Park, the Detroit RiverWalk has what educators, city planners, business leaders, and parents want—unique natural resources that can enhance quality of life, contribute to ecosystem health and healthful living, and nourish our sense of wonder, imagination, and curiosity.

Working in Public–Private Partnerships to Ensure Collective Success

Cities, like Detroit, have always been cradles of culture, technology, and commerce, where history's most luminous minds and civilizations converged (Sadik-Khan and Solomonow 2016). However, cities are also well known for their complex systems of governance and decision making. That is why it is often so difficult to bring about large-scale social change. Kania and Kramer (2011) have shown that large-scale social change, including waterfront redevelopment and urban revitalization, requires broad cross-sector coordination, yet frequently the focus remains on isolated intervention of individual organizations. To address this challenge, Kania and Kramer have proposed a framework that includes five conditions for collective success: a common agenda for collective results, a common measurement system, mutually reinforcing activities, continuous communication, and necessary and sufficient facilitation (table 14). Research has shown that achieving these five conditions results in true alignment among public and private partners, and powerful results. In many respects, the Detroit RiverFront Conservancy has used

TABLE 14. Five Conditions for Collective Success in Large-Scale Projects as Defined by Kania and Kramer (2011), with Examples from the Detroit Riverfront Conservancy

CONDITION	DESCRIPTION	DETROIT RIVERWALK EXAMPLE
Develop Common Agenda for Collective Results	Develop a shared vision for change, one that includes a common understanding of the problem and a joint approach to solving it	In 2002, Detroit's mayor assembled a thirty-four–member East Riverfront Study Group and charged them with developing a revitalization strategy for Detroit's east riverfront. In 2003, the conservancy was created as a nonprofit organization to oversee the creation of a beautiful, exiting, safe, accessible, world-class gathering place for all. Its board of directors is made up of over forty key leaders representing a broad cross-section of public and private organizations throughout Michigan. Substantial efforts were made to ensure an inclusive planning process, one where all voices were heard and factored in. The vision was presented and stakeholder input obtained in nearly one hundred meetings attended by over four thousand people. Community design workshops attracted over six hundred people. Conservancy staff continuously strive to make sure that there is a common understanding of problems and a shared responsibility for solving them.
Develop Shared Measurement System	Ensure agreement among stakeholders on how outcomes will be measured (monitoring) and the frequency of reporting	The conservancy staff annually reports on progress relative to key indicators. In addition, special reports have been prepared that quantify economic and environmental benefits.
Ensure Mutually Reinforcing Activities	Stakeholders must work together to ensure complementary and reinforcing activities	The conservancy has worked closely with public, private, and nongovernmental partners to ensure complementary and reinforcing activities that achieve shared community, economic, and environmental benefits. Considerable efforts are placed on working with and through partners on programming activities.

Ensure Continuous Communication	Communication must be continuous to build trust among stakeholders, ensure transparency, and reach agreement on what actions are needed	Communication is undertaken through a variety of mechanisms, including presentations to stakeholder groups, news releases, media events, annual reports, leadership reports, newsletters, specialty publications, websites, workshops, neighborhood and community forums, etc.
Ensure Necessary Facilitation	Need one organization to be the facilitator and serve as the secretariat, and to create the framework and conditions for collective success	The conservancy functions as the lead facilitator and secretariat on all issues pertaining to the riverfront. However, it seeks out technical assistance where and when necessary. This includes new private developments adjacent to the RiverWalk. The conservancy participates in both public and private partnerships for economic development programs that fit the organization's vision for the waterfront and adjacent communities. Its role varies based on the how the project impacts the conservancy's strategic goals and objectives.

this framework. The key for the Detroit RiverFront Conservancy is to continue to achieve collective success with its many partners. One area of improvement might be in developing a shared measuring system. This could be accomplished by the conservancy working with its partners on indicator reporting every three to five years where data and information on key social, economic, and environmental indicators are compiled and evaluated against measurable targets and benchmarks. Such a framework might be useful to other comparable waterfront initiatives working with many partners to bring about large-scale change.

Continue to Be a Learning Organization

Education is the key to the long-term change in the way people understand and value the places they call home and the ecosystems within which they live. Solutions to problems arise out of cooperative learning. Cooperative learning can be described as common learning that involves stakeholders working in teams to accomplish a common goal, under conditions that involve both positive interdependence (all stakeholders cooperate to complete a task) and individual and group accountability (each stakeholder is responsible for the complete final outcome) (Hartig, Zarull, and Law 1998). Such cooperative learning is essential to address the sustainable development paradigm shift underway.

Clearly, the Detroit RiverFront Conservancy must continue to be a learning organization. One story from the early days of the conservancy is worth telling. In 2001, during the early work of greenway planning, the consulate general of Canada and his staff in Detroit took a group of waterfront leaders from Detroit, including Detroit mayor Dennis Archer, Peter Stroh, Matt Cullen, and John Hartig, to Toronto, Ontario, to learn from their experiences in creating their waterfront trail. The Waterfront Regeneration Trust was the key champion and facilitator of helping municipalities, private interests, and other stakeholders rediscover the value and attractiveness of the water's edge and awaken its citizenry to the potential of the waterfront to lead economic as well as environmental renewal. And this was being done in Canada's largest city with over five million people. The Waterfront Trail opened in 1995, showcasing a 217-mile, virtually continuous trail along the Lake Ontario shoreline. It literally connected hundreds of parks, historic and cultural sites, wildlife habitats, and recreation areas.

The process used by the trust was crystallized in one word—regeneration (Crombie 1992). Increasing public access to the lakefront was a top priority. The trust adopted nine principles to guide decision making for making Toronto a healthier and more sustainable city: clean, green, connected, open, accessible, useable, diverse, affordable, and attractive (Crombie 1992). Toronto's implementation strategy included:

- adopting an ecosystem approach and the nine principles above;

- adjusting plans to ensure they reflect the ecosystem approach and nine principles;
- securing intergovernmental commitments and agreements on what needs to be done, the priorities, who does what, and time frame for actions;
- consolidating capital budgets and pooling resources as necessary to move projects forward;
- creating the framework and conditions for private-sector involvement, and capitalizing on its enterprise, initiative, creativity, and capability for investment; and
- establishing public–private partnerships.

This 2001 trip to the Waterfront Regeneration Trust in Toronto was an important learning and bench-marking experience for Detroit leaders. In fact, in many respects the Detroit RiverFront Conservancy was modeled, in part, after the approach taken by Toronto's Waterfront Regeneration Trust. It is interesting to note that today the key initiative of the Waterfront Regeneration Trust, the Great Lakes Waterfront Trail, stretches over one thousand miles along the shores of Lake Ontario, Lake Erie, Lake St. Clair, Lake Huron, and the St. Clair, Detroit, Niagara, and St. Lawrence rivers. When the Detroit and Winsor greenways get linked by a dedicated bicycle lane on the Gordie Howe Bridge (scheduled to open in 2024), as called for in the Canada–U.S. Greenways Vision Map, then Toronto's greenways will be linked with Detroit's greenways. In many respects we will then have come full circle to our 2001 collaboration with Toronto.

The Detroit RiverFront Conservancy must continue to be a learning organization and reach out to other successful riverfront conservancies to explore new creative ideas and best practices. Perhaps it would be advantageous to establish sister relationships with such organizations and facilitate a regular exchange of staff and thinking to help ensure continuous improvement.

Continue Meaningful Community Engagement

The Detroit RiverFront Conservancy has done an outstanding job of community engagement. The goal should be for the RiverWalk to become part of the community fabric. The conservancy needs to continue to practice the philosophy of working with and for citizens and stakeholder groups. It must engage people where they are at and in their own space, and facilitate good decisions that meet the needs and aspirations of all stakeholders. It needs to fulfill the role of convener, facilitator, and honest broker for all riverfront stakeholders.

To become part of the community fabric, the Detroit RiverFront Conservancy should:

- encourage more people to volunteer for the many meaningful jobs of the Detroit RiverWalk and make a difference;
- expand efforts to get more people to know their Detroit RiverWalk through education, service learning, and other programs;
- encourage more people to try something new on the Detroit RiverWalk;
- keep telling the story and getting the message out;
- communicate and celebrate successes as much as possible;
- involve children in all activities from on-the-ground work to press conferences and celebrating successes;
- offer more meaningful opportunities for schools, block clubs, churches, businesses, and other community organizations to meaningfully participate in the programming and stewardship of the RiverWalk;
- continue to experiment with public–private partnerships to complete the RiverWalk;
- build capacity, trust, and relationships (remember it is all about relationships); and
- have fun in everything it does.

Continuously Improve the Detroit RiverWalk as a Magical Place

The Detroit RiverWalk is a magical place where the water meets the land and people can reconnect with nature and other people. Experience has shown that creating riverfront greenways and vistas, reintroducing residents to river history and geography, establishing unique conservation places linked by greenways and blueways (i.e., canoe and kayak trails), promoting ecotourism, offering creative programming, and championing green developments all help create a sense of place that can foster a stewardship ethic and civic-mindedness (Hartig 2010).

One simple, practical thing that could be done is to better and more clearly communicate the incredible history of Detroit along its riverfront. These Detroit River stories include Native Americans, the fur trade, the Underground Railroad, shipbuilding, automobiles, and more. Each has impacted our nation and indeed the world. They truly are unique and make Detroit exceptional. The Detroit RiverFront Conservancy needs to mold these stories into a compelling message that helps educate and inspire visitors, attract and retain young people and the creative class, and enhance community pride. There are also other things that should be done to continuously improve the RiverWalk as a magical place:

- ensure that walkable urbanism (i.e., an urban design movement that strives for walkable neighborhoods that contain a wide range of housing and job types) continues to inform decision making, including the RiverWalk, the Joe Louis Greenway, and other connections to neighborhoods
- create more greenway connections to neighborhoods, other key city and regional greenway trails, and other centers of cultural and economic activity
- establish more transportation options like water taxis, a Windsor–Detroit ferry, and shuttle buses

- ensure proper way-finding signage
- expand programming through partnerships to ensure the RiverWalk is a year-round destination of choice
- offer more multiple programming and dining options for family visits.

The important point is that the Detroit RiverFront Conservancy and its partners must continue to create an excitement and buzz about visiting, recreating, and relaxing along the Detroit RiverWalk, and must continue to encourage visitors to share their experiences with family and friends.

Continue to Be a Leader in Sustainability

The process of urban waterfront revitalization is part science and part art. We must come to understand places, recognize that everything is connected, ensure broad stakeholder participation, integrate processes, form partnerships, become more proactive, and strive for sustainability (Hartig 2010). For all cities and the ecosystems within which they reside, sustainability is the long-term challenge. With enterprising spirit, excitement for living, working, and playing along waterfronts, and a can-do attitude, cities can meet this sustainability challenge (Hartig 2010).

The United Nations Agenda 21 (1992) articulated a vision of sustainable development as a holistic concept addressing four dimensions of society: economic development (including the end of extreme poverty), social inclusion, environmental sustainability, and good governance. The world has at its disposal the tools to achieve sustainability. Cities like Detroit are uniquely positioned to be leaders of sustainable development. Really, there is no alternative to sustainable development.

Humanity stands at a defining moment in history (United Nations 1992). One choice in life is to follow a path toward stewardship of our natural resources and sustainable development (Global Environment Facility 2002). Another choice is for cities to continue to deplete their natural capital, degrade their environments, and impose limitations on the choices available to their children and grandchildren. As the Global Environment Facility (2002) has stated, the legacy is ours to shape.

Clearly, much more needs to be done to achieve our long-term goal of sustainable development. To meet this sustainability challenge we must become a conserver society. The Detroit RiverWalk is evidence of progress toward that long-term goal. The Detroit RiverFront Conservancy must continue to be a leader in sustainability, like Detroit has done on other paradigm shifts, and be a model for others to follow. The conservancy must also continue to form public–private partnerships that complete the RiverWalk in a manner that models sustainability. Clearly, education for sustainable development can empower people to change the way they think about and work toward a sustainable future. The Detroit RiverFront Conservancy must use its programming and place-making to help create teachable moments that show people how to become a more sustainable community.

There is no doubt that there has been a change in the perception of Detroit and the attitude toward its river. The Detroit River is no longer just a working river that supports commerce and industry and a polluted river in the Rust Belt. It is now seen as an ecological and community asset that provides many beneficial uses that enhance quality of life and increase community pride. This perceptional and attitudinal change has been essential to achieving river revival thus far and to laying the foundation for meeting the sustainability challenge.

Concluding Remarks

Martin Luther King Jr. taught us by word and example that any movement or culture will fail if it cannot paint a picture of a world where people want to go. The Detroit RiverFront Conservancy and its many partners have painted a superb and appealing picture of Detroit's riverfront in its vision that seeks to "transform Detroit's international riverfront—the face of the city—into a beautiful, exciting, safe, accessible world-class gathering place for all" (2018).

Today, the Detroit RiverWalk has become the city's most attractive feature. The Detroit RiverFront Conservancy has created a new waterfront porch for both people and wildlife. It is the new symbol of beauty and hope. It is open every day, free, welcoming to all, and rapidly becoming a major Michigan tourism asset. The Detroit RiverWalk may, in fact, be one of the most diverse places in southeast Michigan, with visitors of all nationalities, races, cultures, and income levels. On any given day you can see families on bikes, athletes, women wearing saris and hijabs, businesspeople in suits, children playing, and people just getting to know other people. This international waterfront is also an important symbol of our friendship with Canada.

In 2016 the Detroit RiverFront Conservancy celebrated the completion of the first phase of its capital campaign, raising $163 million for the Detroit RiverWalk. The next phase will have to complete the former Uniroyal portion of the Detroit RiverWalk, the west riverfront, and other strategic connections to neighborhoods, and to ensure long-term operation, maintenance, and stewardship. Again, the first phase of the capital campaign resulted in more than $1 billion of economic benefits, and the return on investment for the second phase is projected to be even higher. High priority must be placed on making sure that the Detroit RiverWalk is clean, safe, and accessible; a gathering place where people get to know one another; connected by greenways, shuttles, street cars, bike share, water taxis, and other transportation options; green, respects biodiversity, and biophilic; authentic and celebrates Detroit history and culture; and an inclusive destination where all people feel welcome. Detroit has a long-standing, international reputation for revolutionizing manufacturing and perfecting the automobile. It is also well known for:

- world-class art deco architecture and Gilded Age mansions that led many to refer to Detroit as the "Paris of the West";
- being welcoming to immigrants and migrants seeking jobs and a better life; and
- brewing of Stroh's beer and the production of one of the nation's oldest soft drinks called Vernors ginger ale that has a tangy, ginger flavor with a touch of vanilla and carbonation.

However, for over a half century Detroit was often viewed as a symbol of urban decay and the Rust Belt. It is now rapidly gaining an international reputation for its tenacious and ongoing fight back, with artists and entrepreneurs flocking there to be part of a new generation of startups and local businesses focused on technology, commerce, entertainment, and more. The Detroit RiverWalk is playing a complementary and reinforcing role in Detroit's comeback, and the city's future is brighter because of it. For many, the Detroit RiverWalk is physical, concrete, visual proof that Detroit is staging a comeback.

We must continue to make the Detroit RiverWalk a gathering place for all with benefits to all. Detroit has a long history of technological innovation, commerce, and culture that has impacted the world. It now has the ability to be a critical leader of sustainable redevelopment, pivoting, as it has done at each previous paradigm shift, to redefine itself and lead the nation and world down a more sustainable path.

It would be fortuitous to view the Detroit RiverWalk as a commons, owned by no one and available to all who must be involved in its stewardship. As Aldo Leopold noted in his land ethic, we all need to consider ourselves part of the natural community and not separate from it. For only through becoming a more ecologically literate society can we develop the requisite land ethic required to become stewards of the place we call home and to ensure we pass this on as a gift to future generations.

Epilogue

Detroit was the epicenter of the fur trade era, an unparalleled leader of shipbuilding for one hundred years, the Silicon Valley of the industrial age, and the unquestioned leader of the arsenal of democracy. This unique history shows that Detroit is a city of innovation, resilience, and leadership in responding to paradigm shifts. Detroit now must pivot once again and reinvent itself, as it has done at each previous paradigm shift, to become a leader of sustainable redevelopment.

Detroit—from the expanding U.S. frontier to the birth of the Industrial Revolution, to the arsenal of democracy to the soundtrack of the civil rights movement—has been at the center of the American experience. We are tough, gritty, tenacious, and hard working. Detroiters are builders, engineers, and artists; makers of things and writers of songs. Detroit matters because Detroit represents the creative ingenuity that is the basis of American resilience.   —*Matt Seeger*

As noted in chapter 1, during Detroit's arsenal of democracy era all civilian manufacturing capability was converted to military production to help win World War II. In fact, during 1943 and 1944 no cars were built in Detroit. Following World War II, Detroit entered a postwar boom when pent-up consumer demand for automobiles mushroomed. By 1950 the nation's automobile production exceeded eight million vehicles (Martelle 2012). That same year Detroit's population peaked at nearly 1.9 million people. Since then Detroit experienced considerable loss of population and industry, rising unemployment, increased cost of living, decreased access to city services, and increased crime. This decline was attributed to economic (e.g., automobile company decisions to decentralize and build factories closer to regional customer bases), social (e.g., racism), and political (e.g., lack of sound urban planning) reasons (Martelle 2012). To many, Detroit had become the preeminent example of urban decline. Since 1960, Detroit experienced a 60 percent loss in population and considerable losses in industrial jobs. During this era, it became a city more often characterized by hardship than success. This industrial and demographic decline, and the social and economic problems that went with it, culminated with Detroit's insolvency and eventual bankruptcy in 2013.

For over a century Detroit had been an industrial town with a working riverfront that supported industry and commerce. Following Detroit's population peak in 1950, there was a gradual regression to fewer people and industries, culminating with much underutilized and undervalued riverfront land. Detroiters had long lost their connection to the Detroit River. In the decades that followed, citizens began calling for greater public access to the Detroit River and for changing the perception of Detroit from that of a Rust Belt city to one that is actively engaged in sustainable redevelopment.

To deny the river is to deny the origin of the city. To rethink the river is to discover a unique opportunity to define urban places, join neighborhoods and communities together, and reconnect us to our landscape and our history. —*Arthur Golding*

Because of Detroit's long industrial history and its growth into the fifth largest city in the United States in 1950, the Detroit River became one of the most polluted rivers in North America by the 1960s. Public outcry over this pollution led to the enactment of many federal and state environmental laws, and the signing of the U.S.–Canada Great Lakes Water Quality Agreement. These regulations and the Great Lakes Water Quality Agreement triggered considerable industrial and municipal pollution prevention and control. Today, the cleanup and recovery of the Detroit River represent one of the single most remarkable ecological recovery stories in North America, with the return of bald eagles, peregrine falcons, osprey, lake sturgeon, lake whitefish, walleye, wild celery, mayflies, and even beaver.

Out of this growing public interest to reconnect to the Detroit River, ecological recovery, and strong public and private support, the Detroit RiverFront Conservancy was created to "transform Detroit's international riverfront—the face of the city—into a beautiful, exciting, safe, accessible world-class gathering place for all" (Detroit RiverFront Conservancy 2018). Today, the conservancy and its partners are transforming their postindustrial waterfront into a new waterfront porch, called the Detroit RiverWalk, that improves quality of life, celebrates Detroit's rich history and culture, protects the environment, strengthens the economy, and inspires many visitors to regain a childlike sense of wonder for the outdoors. This new waterfront porch has become a gathering place for both people and wildlife (figure 49). Nearly three million annual visitors are already using it. Economists have quantified that in the first ten years of the Detroit RiverWalk, there was an over $1 billion return on investment, with the potential for even a greater return in the future.

In great cities, spaces as well as places are designed and built: walking,

SMITHGROUPJJR

FIGURE 49. The Detroit RiverWalk as the new, international, waterfront porch of the city that is a gathering place for both people and wildlife.

> witnessing, being in public, are as much part of the design and purpose
> as is being inside to eat, sleep, make shoes or love or music. The word
> citizen has to do with cities, and the ideal city is organized around
> citizenship—around participation in public life.   —*Rebecca Solnit*

The Detroit RiverWalk is rapidly becoming the iconographic image of Detroit in the twenty-first century and a key supporting element in Detroit's revival. Together, the RiverWalk and a civic-mindedness that must be manifested through seven-day-a-week programming, connections to the neighborhoods and other key centers of economic, entertainment, and community activities, and the successful establishment of a sense of place and stewardship can help Detroit reestablish itself as one of the great waterfront cities in the world.

> It is a wholesome and necessary thing for us to turn again to the earth

and in the contemplation of her beauties to know the sense of wonder and humility. —*Rachel Carson*

The Detroit RiverWalk has also become an urban getaway for outdoor recreation. Because of close-to-home greenways, blueways, flyways, world-class fishing, and more, Detroit residents don't have to drive four or more hours up north to get an exceptional outdoor recreational experience.

Nature is not a place to visit. It is home. —*Gary Snyder*

Some ask why should people care about building the Detroit River-Walk in Motown? One simple answer is that it is one of the largest urban waterfront redevelopment projects in the United States, and if such waterfront redevelopment can be done in Motown, with all its well-known challenges, it can be done elsewhere. A second answer has three parts:

- Cities are the creative engines that drive innovation and growth, and Detroit has demonstrated time and again that its creativity, innovation, and work ethic can impact the nation and world.
- It is an economic and political fact that we are all inextricably linked and that Detroit is an indispensable part of the American economy and culture.
- Detroit has always been there to help meet the needs of the nation and world, and now Detroit needs the nation to help Detroit create the America for tomorrow—until we see a renaissance of Detroit we cannot fully realize the American Dream.

Why Detroit? Because it's big enough to matter in the world, but small enough that you can matter in it. —*Jeanette Pierce*

A third answer is that it protects natural capital, improves quality of life, enhances competitive advantage, and helps develop the next generation of conservationists and sustainability entrepreneurs in urban areas because that is now where 80 percent of all U.S. people live.

Every great city has a place where people can gather and all are welcome. In Detroit, it is the Detroit RiverWalk. Even though it is not yet fully complete, it has already captured the hearts and minds of millions of people. During major sporting events and civic celebrations, the RiverWalk is frequently featured on television as the city's new, remarkable, waterfront gathering place for people and wildlife. More remains to be done to complete the RiverWalk, and the full story has yet to be written. The Detroit RiverFront Conservancy and its partners must continue to have a sense of urgency to complete the Detroit RiverWalk from Belle Isle's MacArthur Bridge to the Ambassador Bridge to Canada, and to establish key linkages to neighborhoods. But so much has already been done that provides a foretaste of what is yet to come. I invite you to come visit the Detroit RiverWalk and see and feel the excitement. You may even want to sit a while on our new front porch, contemplate the beauty of the Detroit River and this city, and ponder it with a childlike sense of wonder.

Rivers flow not past, but through us; tingling, vibrating, exciting every cell and fiber in our bodies, making them glide and sing.   —*John Muir*

References

Alberta, T. 2014. "Is Dan Gilbert Detroit's New Superhero?" *Atlantic*, February 28.

American Automotive Policy Council. 2015. *State of the U.S. Automotive Industry, 2015*. Washington, DC: American Automotive Policy Council. http://www.americanautocouncil.org.

Appel, L.M., J.A. Craves, M.K. Smith, B. Weir, and J.M. Zawiskie. 2002. "Urban Wildlife." In *Explore Our Natural World: A Biodiversity Atlas of the Lake Huron to Lake Erie Corridor*, edited by Mary Kehoe Smith and Bob Weir. Detroit: Wildlife Habitat Council.

Baycan, T. 2011. "Creative Cities: Context and Perspectives." In *Sustainable City and* Thompson *Creativity: Promoting Creative Urban Initiatives*, edited by L.F. Girard, T. Baycan, and P. Nijkamp. Burlington, VT: Ashgate.

Beatly, T. 2011. *Biophilic Cities: Integrating Nature into Urban Design and Planning*. Washington, DC: Island Press.

Becher, C.K. and J.H. Hartig. 2017. *Peregrine falcon reproduction in southeast Michigan*. Lansing, MI: Michigan Department of Natural Resources.

Bein, L., 2012. "In the Archives: From Cordwood to Cavier." *Ann Arbor Chronicle,* February 28.

Bennion, D.H., and M.A. Manny. 2011. *Construction of Shipping Channels in the Detroit River: History and Environmental Consequences.* Scientific Investigations Report 2011-5122. Reston, VA: U.S. Geological Survey.

Best, D. and E. Wilke. 2007. "Bald Eagle Reproductive Success." In *State of the Strait: Status and Trends of Key Indicators,* edited by J.H. Hartig, M.A. Zarull, J.J.H. Ciborowski, J.E. Gannon, E. Wilke, G. Norwood, and A. Vincent, 267–75. Great Lakes Institute for Environmental Research, Occasional Publication No. 5. Windsor, Ont.: University of Windsor.

Binelli, M. 2013. *Detroit City Is the Place to Be: An Afterlife of an American Metropolis.* New York: Henry Holt.

Bogue, M.B. 2000. *Fishing the Great Lakes: An Environmental History, 1783–1933.* Madison: University of Wisconsin Press.

Bohl, C.C. 2002. *Place Making: Developing Town Centers, Main Streets, and Urban Villages.* Washington, DC: Urban Land Institute.

Bowerman, W.W., J.P. Giesy, D.A. Best, and V.J. Kramer. 1995. "A Review of Factors Affecting Productivity of Bald Eagles in the Great Lakes Region: Implications for Recovery." *Environmental Health Perspectives* 103 (Suppl. 4): 51–59.

Bowerman, W.W., D.A. Best, T.G. Grubb, G.M. Zimmerman, and J.P. Giesy. 1998. "Trends of Contaminants and Effects in Bald Eagles of the Great Lakes Basin." *Environmental Monitoring and Assessment* 53: 197–212.

Bowerman, W.W., A.S. Roe, M.J. Gilbertson, D.A. Best, J.G. Sikarskie, R.S. Mitchell, and C.L. Summer. 2002. "Using Bald Eagles to Indicate the Health of the Great Lakes' Environment." *Lakes & Reservoirs: Research and Management* 7: 183–87.

Bowker, J.M., J. Bergstrom, and J.K. Gill. 2004. *The Virginia Creeper Trail: An Assessment of User Demographics, Preferences, and Economics.* Richmond: Virginia Department of Conservation and Recreation.

Bruntland, G. 1987. *Our Common Future.* World Commission on Environment and Development. Oxford: Oxford University Press.

Bradford, N. 2002. "Why Cities Matter: Policy Research Perspectives for Canada." Canadian Policy Research Networks Discussion Paper No. F23. Ottawa, Canada.

Bradford, N. 2004. "Creative Cites: Structured Policy Dialogue Report." Creative Cities: Structured Policy Dialogue Report F45. Ottawa, Canada.

Business Leaders for Michigan, Public Sector Accountants, and Sustainable Water Works. 2015. *Michigan Natural Resources Business Plan: Leveraging Our Assets to Make Michigan a Top Ten State.* Lansing, MI.

Card, J., 2013. *Ten Great Cities for Waterfowlers.* Memphis, TN: Ducks Unlimited. Http://www.ducks.org/hunting/destinations/10-great-cities-for-waterfowlers.

Carson, R. 1962. *Silent Spring.* Boston: Houghton Mifflin.

Carver, E. 2013. *Birding in the United States: A Demographic and Economic Analysis.* Arlington, VA: U.S. Fish and Wildlife Service.

Castel, A. 1998. "Old Pap: Michigan's Top Civil War General. *Michigan History* 82 (4): 18–26.

Caswell, N.M., D.L. Peterson, B.A. Manny, and G.W. Kennedy. 2004. "Spawning by Lake Sturgeon (*Acipenser fulvescens*) in the Detroit River." *Journal of Applied Ichthyology* 20: 1-6.

Chappell, S.A.K. 2007. *Chicago's Urban Nature: A Guide to the City's Architecture and Landscape.* Chicago: University of Chicago Press.

Chartier, Allen. 2007. Hotspots Near You: Belle Isle Park, Detroit, Michigan. BirdWatchingDaily.com.

Chiotti, J., L. Mohr, M. Thomas, J. Boase, and B. Manny. 2012. *Lake Sturgeon Population Demographics in the St. Clair-Detroit River System, 1996-2012.* American Fisheries Society 142nd Annual Meeting (August 9th), Minneapolis-St. Paul, Minnesota, USA.Ciborowski, J. 2007. "*Hexagenia* Density and Distribution in the Detroit River." In *State of the Strait: Status and Trends of Key Indicators*, edited by J.H. Hartig, M.A. Zarull, J.J.H. Ciborowski, J.E. Gannon, E. Wilke, G. Norwood, and A. Vincent, 181–88. Great Lakes Institute for Environmental Research Occasional Publication No. 5. Windsor, Ont.: University of Windsor. ISSN 1715-3980.

Colborn, T. 1991. "Epidemiology of Great Lakes Bald Eagles." *Journal of Toxicology and Environmental Health* 33: 395–453.

Cornell, G.L. 2003. "American Indians at Wawiiatanong: An Early American History of Indigenous Peoples at Detroit." In *Honoring Our Detroit River: Caring for Our Home,* edited by J.H. Hartig, 9–22. Bloomfield Hills, MI: Cranbrook Institute of Science.

Cowles, G. 1975. "Return of the River." *Michigan Natural Resources Magazine* 44 (1): 2-6.

Cox, N. 1999. *Detroit's New Front Porch: A Riverfront Greenway in Southwest Detroit.* Detroit: Rails-to-Trails Conservancy.

Crombie, D. 1992. *Regeneration: Toronto's Waterfront and the Sustainable City.* Toronto: Queen Printer of Ontario.

CSL International. 2013. *Economic Impact Study: Detroit Riverfront.* Detroit: Detroit Riverfront Conservancy.

Davis, M.W.R. 2007. *Detroit's Wartime Industry: Arsenal of Democracy.* Chicago: Arcadia Publishing.

Dempsey, J. 2011. *Michigan and the Civil War: A Great and Bloody Sacrifice.* Charlestown, SC: Hickory Press.

Detroit Free Press. 1903. "A Day with the Sturgeon Fishers of Fox Island," July 12.

Detroit Future City. 2012. *Detroit Strategic Framework Plan.* Detroit, MI: Island Press.

Detroit RiverFront Conservancy. 2018. Vision & Mission. Http://www.detroitriverfront.org/our-story/vision-mission.

Dimon, J. 2015. "How to Rev the Growth Engine." *Wall Street Journal,* September 16.

Dunbar, W.F. 1965. *Michigan: A History of the Wolverine State.* Grand Rapids, MI: W.B. Eerdmans.

Dunbar, W.F., and G.S. May. 1995. *Michigan: A History of the Wolverine State.* 3d ed. Grand Rapids, MI: William B. Eerdmans.

Dunnigan, B.L. 2001. *Frontier Metropolis: Picturing Early Detroit, 1701–1838.* Detroit: Wayne State University Press.

Eastern Market Corporation. 2016. *Eastern Market Strategy: 2025.* Detroit, MI.

Farmer, S. 1890. *History of Detroit and Wayne County and Early Michigan*. Detroit: Silas Farmer.

Florida, R. 2002. *The Rise of the Creative Class: And How It's Transforming Work, Leisure, Community and Everyday Life*. New York: Basic Books.

Freud, D. 2017. "Machine Learning: Evolution in the Age of Acceleration." *D!gitalist Magazine*, August 3.

Fromm, E. 1973. *The Anatomy of Human Destructiveness*. New York: Henry Holt.

Gallagher, J. 2010. *Reimaging Detroit: Opportunities for Redefining an American City*. Detroit: Wayne State University Press.

Gallagher, J. 2017. "How Detroit's Tallest Skyscraper Would Be Built at Former Hudson's Site." *Detroit Free Press*, March 2.

Gavrilovich, P., and B. McGraw. 2000. *The Detroit Almanac: 300 Years of Life in the Motor City*. Detroit: Detroit Free Press.

Glaeser, E. 2011. *Triumph of the City: How Our Greatest Invention Makes Us Richer, Smarter, Greener, Healthier, and Happier*. London: Macmillan Publishers.

Global Environment Facility. 2002. *The Sustainability Challenge: An Action Agenda for the Global Environment*. Washington, DC.

Goodyear, C.D., T.A. Edsall, D.M. Ormsby-Dempsey, G.D. Moss, and P.E. Polanski. 1982. *Atlas of Spawning and Nursery Areas of Great Lakes Fishes*. FWS/OBS-82/52. Volumes 1–14. Washington, DC: U.S. Fish and Wildlife Service.

Great Lakes Commission. 2007. *Great Lakes Recreational Boating' Economic Punch*. Ann Arbor, MI.

Hardin, T. 2013. "Why Detroit Does Matter?" *Cultural Weekly*, August 14.

Hartig, J.H. 2014. *Bringing Conservation to Cities: Lessons from Building the Detroit River International Wildlife Refuge*. Ecovision World Monograph Series. Burlington, Ont.: Aquatic Ecosystem Health and Management Society.

——. 2010. *Burning Rivers: Revival of Four Urban-Industrial Rivers that Caught on Fire*. Ecovision World Monograph Series, Aquatic Ecosystem Health and Management Society. Essex, UK: Multi-Science Publishing.

——. 2003. *Honoring Our Detroit River: Caring for Our Home*. Bloomfield Hills, MI: Cranbrook Institute of Science.

————. 1983. "Lake St. Clair: Since the 'Mercury Crisis.'" *Water Spectrum* 15: 18–25.

Hartig, J.H., and T. Stafford. 2003. "The Public Outcry over Oil Pollution of the Detroit River." In *Honoring Our Detroit River: Caring for Our Home*, edited by J.H. Hartig, 69–78. Bloomfield Hills, MI: Cranbrook Institute of Science.

Hartig, J.H., and M.C. Wallace. 2015. "Creating World-Class Gathering Places for People and Wildlife along the Detroit Riverfront, Michigan, USA." *Sustainability 7:* 15073–98.

Hartig J.H., R.S. Robinson, and M.A. Zarull. 2010. "Designing a Sustainable Future through Creation of North America's only International Wildlife Refuge." *Sustainability* 2: 3110–28.

Hartig, J.H., M.A. Zarull, J.J.H. Ciborowski, J.E. Gannon, E. Wilke, G. Norwood, and A. Vincent. 2009. "Long-term Ecosystem Monitoring and Assessment of the Detroit River and Western Lake Erie." *Environmental Monitoring and Assessment* 158: 87–104.

Hartig, J.H., M.A. Zarull, and N.L. Law. 1998. "An Ecosystem Approach to Great Lakes Management: Practical Steps." *Journal of Great Lakes Research* 24 (3): 739-50.

Hartman, W.L. 1972. "Lake Erie: Effects of Exploitation, Environmental Changes, and New Species on the Fishery Resources." *Journal of the Fisheries Research Board of Canada* 29: 899–912.

Hatcher, H. 1945. *Lake Erie*. New York: Bobbs-Merrill.

Haub, C. 2007. *World Population Data Sheet*. Washington, DC: Population Reference Bureau.

Hemming, B. 2005. "The Detroit Riverfront Conservancy: A Public–Private Partnership Striving to Reclaim the Detroit River." *Golden Gate University Law Review* 35 (3): 1–16.

Holli, M.G., ed. 1976. *Detroit*. New York: New Viewpoints.

Hudgins, B. 1946. "Old Detroit: Drainage and Land Forms." *Michigan History Magazine* 30 (2): 348–68.

Huffman, J.L. 1951. *Detroit and the Civil War*. Detroit: Wayne State University Press.

Interagency Task Force for Detroit/Wayne County Riverfront Development. 1976. *Partners for Progress: The Land & the River. Office of Economic Expansion.* Detroit: Michigan Department of Commerce.

Jacobs, J. 1961. *The Death and Life of Great American Cities.* New York: Random House.

Johnson, I.A. 1919. *The Michigan Fur Trade.* Lansing: Michigan Historical Commission.

Kania, J., and M. Kramer. 2011. "Collective Impact." *Stanford Social Innovation Review.* Winter: 36–41. http://ssir.org/images/articles/2011_WI_Feature_Kania.pdf

Kayle, K., K. Oldenburg, C. Murray, J. Francis, and J. Markham. 2015. *Lake Erie Walleye Management Plan: 2015–2019.* Ann Arbor, MI: Lake Erie Committee, Great Lakes Fishery Commission.

Klug, T.A. 2002. *Dry Dock Engine Works.* Washington, DC: Historic American Engineering Record, National Park Service.

Kovats, Z.E., J.J.H. Ciborowski, and L.D. Corkum. 1996. "Inland Dispersal of Adult Aquatic Insects." *Freshwater Biology* 36: 265–76.

Kuhn, T.S. 1962. *The Structure of Scientific Revolutions.* Chicago: University of Chicago Press.

Lake Erie Walleye Task Group. 2005. *Report for 2004 by the Lake Erie Walleye Task Group.* Ann Arbor, MI: Lake Erie Committee, Great Lakes Fishery Commission.

———. 2017. *Executive Summary Report.* Ann Arbor, MI: Lake Erie Committee, Great Lakes Fishery Commission.

Kuras, A. 2014. "Jeanette Pierce." *Detroit Urban Innovation Exchange,* January 17.

Leach, J.H., 1999. "Lake Erie: Passages Revisited." In *State of Lake Erie: Past, Present and Future,* edited by M. Munawar, T. Edsall, and I.F. Munawar, 5–22. Leiden: Backhuys Publishers.

Levanen, A.J. 2000. "The River's Edge: A History of the Detroit Waterfront." *Telescope* (Great Lakes Maritime Institute) (March–April): 6–9.

LewAllen, D. 2016. "Eastern Market's 10-Year Expansion Plan Would Generate Millions in Investment and Additional Jobs." WXYZ Detroit, May 17.

Louv, R., 2005. *Last Child in the Woods: Saving Our Children from Nature-Deficit Disorder.* Chapel Hill, NC: Algonquin Books.

Lydon, M., and A. Garcia. 2015. *Tactical Urbanism: Short-Term Action for Long-Term Change.* Washington, DC: Island Press.

McKinsey Global Institute. 2012. *Urban America: U.S. Cities in the Global Economy.* New York: McKinsey Global Institute.

Malnor, B., and C. L. Malnor. 2009. *Champions of the Wilderness.* Nevada City, CA: Dawn Publications.

Manny, B.A., 2003. "Setting Priorities for Conserving and Rehabilitating Detroit River Habitats." In *Honoring Our Detroit River: Caring for Our Home*, edited by J.H. Hartig, 79–90. Bloomfield Hills, MI: Cranbrook Institute of Science.

Martelle, S. 2012. *Detroit: A Biography.* Chicago: Chicago Review Press.

Metro Detroit Nature Network. 2017. *Metropolitan Detroit's Bird Agenda.* Grosse Ile, MI: Detroit River International Wildlife Refuge.

Michigan Department of Natural Resources. 1998. *Osprey Recovery Plan.* Lansing: State of Michigan.

Muir, D. 2000. *Reflections on Bullough's Pond: Economy and Ecosystem in New England.* Hanover, NH: University of New England Press.

Muir, J. 1912. *The Yosemite.* New York: Century Co.

National Association of Realtors and National Association of Home Builders. 2002. *Consumer's Survey on Smart Choices for Home Buyers.* Washington, DC.

National Marine Manufacturers Association. 2014. "2014 Recreational Boating: Statistical Abstract." Chicago.

Nicholls, S., and J. Crompton. 2005. "The Impact of Greenways on Property Values: Evidence from Austin, Texas." *Journal of Leisure Research* 37 (3): 321–41.

Nivin, S. 2014. *Impact of the San Antonio River Walk.* San Antonio: San Antonio River Authority and the Pasio del Rio Association.

Nolan, J. 2000. "How the Detroit River Shaped Lives and History." *Detroit News.* http://blogs.detroitnews.com/history/1997/02/10/how-the-detroit-river-shaped-lives-and-history.

North American Fur Trade Conference. 1967. "Aspects of the Fur Trade." Paper published by the Conference. St. Paul, MN.

Outdoor Foundation, The. 2015. *2015 Special Report on Paddlesports*. Washington, DC.

Outdoor Industry Association. 2012. *The Outdoor Recreation Economy: Take it Outside for American Jobs and a Strong Economy*. Boulder, CO.

Outdoor Industry Foundation. 2006. *The Active Outdoor Recreation Economy*. Boulder, CO.

Pinho, K. 2014. "Gilbert's Reactions to Detroit Bankruptcy Fining and Ruling Are Steeped in Optimism." *Crain's Business Detroit*, November 7.

Pollock, J.R. 2013. "Bumpkins and Bostonnais: Detroit, 1805–1812." PhD diss. University of Toledo.

Pollstar. 2017. Year End Edition. Fresno, CA.

Postupalsky, S. 1977. "Status of the Osprey in Michigan." In *Transactions of the North American Osprey Research Conference*, edited by J.C. Ogden, 153–65. Washington, DC: U.S. Department of Interior.

Prevost, l'A.A.F. 1746-59. *Histoire generale des voyages*. Paris, France.

Roberts, R.E. 1855. *Sketches of the City of Detroit: Past and Present*. Detroit, MI: R. F. Johnstone & Co.

Reynolds, E. 2011. "Interwhile Uses." *Journal of Urban Regeneration and Renewal* 4 (4): 371–80.

Rock Ventures. 2013. *Opportunity Detroit: A Placemaking Vision for Downtown Detroit*. Detroit, MI.

Roseman, E.F., M. DuFour, J. Pritt, R. DeBruyne, J. Fischer, and D. Bennion. 2017. "Export of Pelagic Fish Larvae from the Detroit River." Paper presented at the Midwest Fish and Wildlife Conference, Feb. 5–8, Lincoln, NE.

Roseman, E.F., G.W. Kennedy, B.A. Manny, J. Boase, and J. McFee. 2012. "Life History Characteristics of a Recovering Lake Whitefish *Coregonus clupeaformis* Stock in the Detroit River, North America." Proceedings of the 10th Coregonid Fishes Symposium. *Advances in Limnology* 63: 477–501.

Roseman, E.F., B. Manny, J. Boase, M. Child, G. Kennedy, J. Craig, K. Soper, and

R. Drouin. 2011. "Lake Sturgeon Response to a Spawning Reef Constructed in the Detroit River." *Journal of Applied Ichthyology* 27 (Suppl. 2): 66–76.

Ryan, B.D. 2012. *Design after Decline: How America Rebuilds Shrinking Cites.* Philadelphia: University of Pennsylvania Press.

Sadik-Khan, J., and S. Solomonow. 2016. *Streetfight: Handbook for an Urban Revolution.* New York: Viking.

Schneekloth, L.H., and R.G. Shibley. 1995. *Placemaking: The Art and Practice of Building Communities.* New York: John Wiley & Sons.

Schloesser, D., and K.A. Krieger. 2007. "Abundance of Burrowing Mayflies in the Western Basin of Lake Erie." In *State of the Strait: Status and Trends of Key Indicators,* edited by J.H. Hartig, M.A. Zarull, J.J.H. Ciborowski, J.E. Gannon, E. Wilke, G. Norwood, and A. Vincent, 189–92. Great Lakes Institute for Environmental Research Occasional Publication No. 5. Windsor, Ont.: University of Windsor.

Schloesser, D., and B.A. Manny. 2007. "Recovery of Wild Celery." In *State of the Strait: Status and Trends of Key Indicators,* edited by J.H. Hartig, M.A. Zarull, J.J.H. Ciborowski, J.E. Gannon, E. Wilke, G. Norwood, and A. Vincent, 160–62. Great Lakes Institute for Environmental Research Occasional Publication No. 5. Windsor, Ont.: University of Windsor. ISSN 1715-3980.

Scott, W.B., and E.J. Crossman. 1973. *Freshwater Fishes of Canada.* Ottawa: Fisheries Research Board of Canada.

Senge, P.M., 1990. *The Fifth Discipline: The Art and Practice of the Learning Organization.* New York: Currency Doubleday Books.

Silberberg, S., K. Lorah, R. Disbrow, and A. Muessig. 2013. *Places in the Making: How Placemaking Builds Places and Communities.* Cambridge, MA: MIT Press.

Solla, S.R. de, D.V.C. Weseloh, K.D. Hughes, and D.J. Moore. 2015. "Forty-Year Decline of Organic Contaminants in Eggs of Herring Gulls (*Larus argentatus*) from the Great Lakes, 1974 to 2013." *Waterbirds* 39 (Suppl. 1): 166–79.

Taylor, P. 2013. *Old Slow Town: Detroit during the Civil War.* Detroit: Wayne State

University Press.

The Editors. 2013. "Why Do Birds Matter?" *National Audubon Society*, August.

Thompson, B. 2016. "Vacant Hudson's Block in Detroit to Be Redeveloped." *MI Headlines*, April 27.

Time. 1965. "Ecology: Time for Transfusion." 86 (8): August 20..

Tobin, J., and H. Jones. 2007. *From Midnight to Dawn: The Last Tracks of the Underground Railroad.* New York: Anchor Book.

Tody, W.H., 1974. "Whitefish, Sturgeon, and the Early Michigan Commercial Fishery." In *Michigan Fisheries Centennial Report, 1873-1973*, 45-60. Lansing: Michigan Department of Natural Resources.

Tordoff, H.B., and P. Redig. 1997. "Midwest Peregrine Falcon Demography, 1982-1995." *Journal of Raptor Research* 31 (4): 339-46.

Trautman, M.B. 1957. *The Fishes of Ohio.* Columbus: Ohio State University Press.

Turney, W.G. 1971. "Mercury Pollution: Michigan's Action Program." *Water Pollution Control Federation* 43 (7): 1427-38.

United Nations. 1992. "Sustainable Development—Agenda 21." Rio de Janerio, June 3-14.

United Nations, Department of Economic and Social Affairs, Population Division. 2014. *World Urbanization Prospects: The 2014 Revision, Highlights* (ST/ESA/SER.A/352). New York.

United Nations, Department of Economic and Social Affairs, Population Division. 2006. *World Urbanization Prospects: The 2005 Revision* (ESA/P/WP/200). New York.

U.S. Census Bureau. 2015. *Quick Facts for Detroit and Michigan.* Washington, DC.

U.S. Department of Health, Education, and Welfare. 1962. *Pollution of the Navigable Water of the Detroit River, Lake Erie and Their Tributaries within the State of Michigan.* Detroit.

U.S. Department of the Interior, U.S. Fish and Wildlife Service, U.S. Department of Commerce, and U.S. Census Bureau. 2011. *2011 National Survey of Fishing, Hunting, and Wildlife-Associated Recreation.* Washington, DC.

U.S. Fish and Wildlife Service. 2013. *Introduction to the Standards of Excellence for Urban National Wildlife Refuges.* Washington, DC.

———. 2011. *Conserving the Future: Wildlife Refuges and the Next Generation.* Arlington, VA: National Wildlife Refuge System.

Urban Land Institute. 2016. *Active Transportation and Real Estate: The Next Frontier.* Washington, DC.

———. 2015. *America in 2015: An Urban Land Institute Survey of Views on Housing, Transportation and Community.* Washington, DC.

Wade, N. 1977. "Thomas S. Kuhn: Revolutionary Theorist of Science." *Science* 197 (4299): 143-54.

Walljasper, J. 2007. *The Great Neighborhood Book: A Do-It-Yourself Guide to Placemaking.* Gabriola Island, BC: New Society Publishers.

Walters, K. 2012. *The Underground Railroad: A Reference Guide.* Santa Barbara, CA: ABC-CLIO.

Waterfront Center. 1999. *Urban Waterfront Manifesto.* Washington, DC.

Wilson, E.O. 1984. *Biophilia: The Human Bond with Other Species.* Cambridge, MA: Harvard University Press.

World Bank. 1998. "Chapter 6." In *World Development Report 1999–2000, Entering the 21st Century: The Changing Development Landscape*, 125–38. Washington, DC.

Wos, J. 2017. "Open Water." *TBD Magazine*, August.

Wright, S., and W.M. Tidd. 1933. "Summary of Limnological Investigations in Western Lake Erie in 1929 and 1930." *Transactions of the American Fisheries Society* 63: 271–85.

Yerkey, J.M., and T. Payne. 2007. "Peregrine Falcon Reproduction in Southeast Michigan." In *State of the Strait: Status and Trends of Key Indicators*, edited by J.H. Hartig, M.A. Zarull, J.J.H. Ciborowski, J.E. Gannon, E. Wilke, G. Norwood, and A. Vincent, 263–66. Great Lakes Institute for Environmental Research Occasional Publication No. 5. Windsor, Ont.: University of Windsor. ISSN 1715-3980.

Zegarac, M., and T.A. Muir. 1996. *A Catalogue of Benefits Associated with Greenspaces and an Analysis of the Effects of Greenspaces on Residential Property Values: A Windsor Case Study.* Ottawa: Environment Canada.

Index

American dream, 183, 188, 190, 194, 217
Arsenal of democracy, 17–18, 28,
    39–40, 150, 183, 187, 190, 193,
    213–14

Biodiversity, 154, 200
Biophilic city, 199–200
ByWays to FlyWays, 155–56, 173

Campus Martius, 80, 83, 123–25
Community Foundation for Southeast
    Michigan, 30, 80, 82, 83, 95, 144
Competitive advantage, 22, 160, 218
Cooperative learning, 196, 198, 204–5

Dequindre Cut, 81, 95–96, 99–100,

128, 145, 173, 199
Detroit Audubon, 155, 170
Detroit Greenways Coalition, 30, 81,
    144–45, 148
Detroit Heritage River Water Trail,
    149–53, 173
Detroit RiverFront Conservancy, 33,
    81, 84–86, 88–89, 94, 102, 104,
    110–14, 116, 134, 142, 144, 146,
    157–58, 160–61, 173, 195, 198–99,
    203–7, 209–11, 215, 218
Detroit River International Wildlife
    Refuge, 30, 148, 153, 197–98
Detroit RiverWalk, 77–117, 133–37,
    141–42, 145, 151, 154, 158, 161–63,
    173, 195–212, 215–18

Eastern Market, 81, 96, 125–30, 145

Ecological recovery, 55–76, 215

Economic benefits, 159–73, 203

Fur trade, 4, 11–12, 28, 35–37, 189, 191, 213

Greenways, 30–31, 41, 80–82, 87, 95–96, 99–100, 111–13, 128, 134–35, 141–48, 163–66, 205–6, 208, 217

Great Lakes Water Quality Agreement, 59, 215

Industrial revolution, 141, 150, 183, 187

Midtown, 96, 130, 145, 178, 184

Motor City or Motown, 1, 6, 16, 51, 107, 178, 184, 186–87, 189, 217

Outdoor Adventure Center, 82, 99–101

Paradigm shift, 9–13, 15, 17, 18, 20, 23, 28, 195, 213

Place-making, 119–39, 162, 200

Polluted river, 6, 55–59, 73–76, 210, 215

Public-private partnerships, 202–4, 206–7, 210

QLINE, 121, 180

Quality of life, 28, 32, 143, 159, 173

Ralph C. Wilson, Jr. Centennial Park, 82, 110–11, 114–15, 136, 199

Renaissance Center, 40, 77–78, 80, 82, 101–4

Rust Belt, 33, 52, 77, 172, 175, 195, 215

Sense of wonder, 154, 202, 215–16, 218

Shipbuilding, 5, 13–15, 50–51, 138, 150, 177

Stormwater, 59, 98, 137, 199

Sustainability or sustainable development, 7, 20–32, 72, 77, 181–82, 195, 209–10, 218

Underground railroad, 37, 80, 150, 189, 191–92

West Riverfront Park. *See* Ralph C. Wilson, Jr. Centennial Park

World War II, 17–20, 39–40, 60, 190, 193